How to Create Math Experts With
Fraction Slices™

Lyle Lee Jenkins & Peggy McLean

I0457559

Splice them together

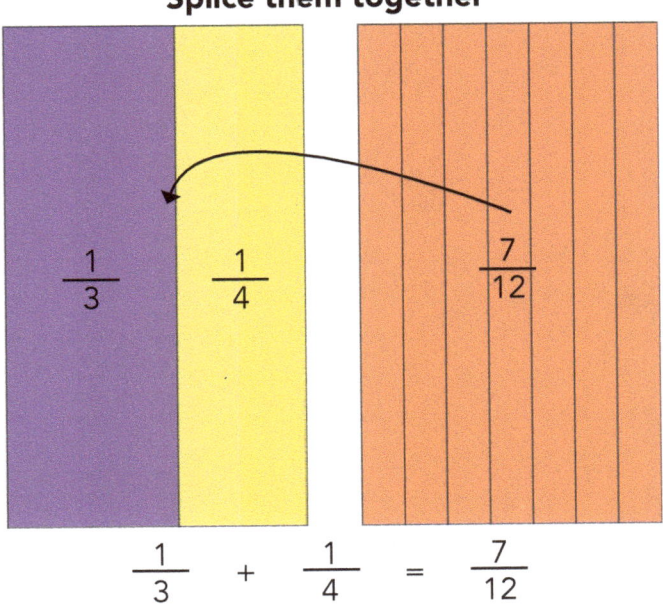

$$\frac{1}{3} + \frac{1}{4} = \frac{7}{12}$$

Cover both pieces with one color.

A concise comp

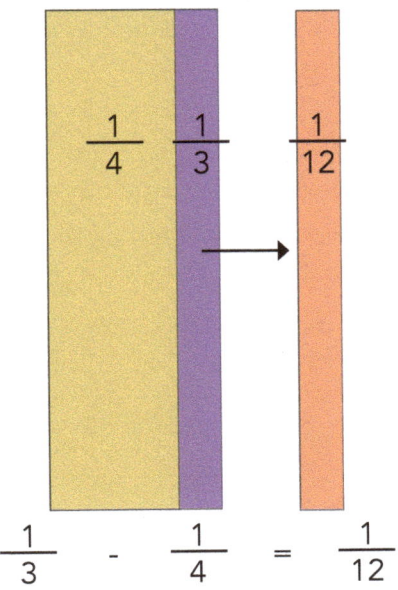

$$\frac{1}{3} - \frac{1}{4} = \frac{1}{12}$$

How much larger is $\frac{1}{3}$ than $\frac{1}{4}$?

Dice them into pieces

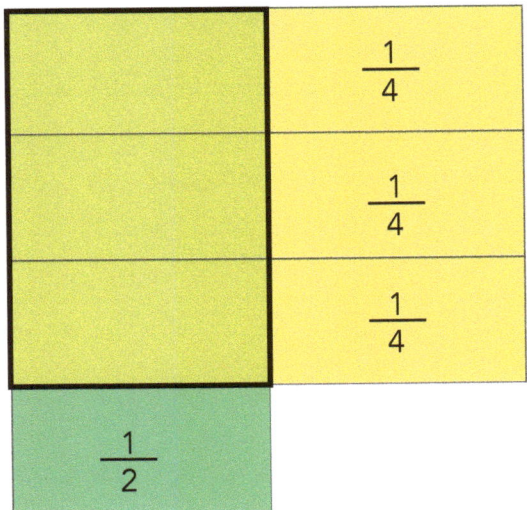

$$\frac{1}{2} \times \frac{3}{4} = \frac{3}{8}$$

Fraction multiplication creates smaller rectangles.

Be precise

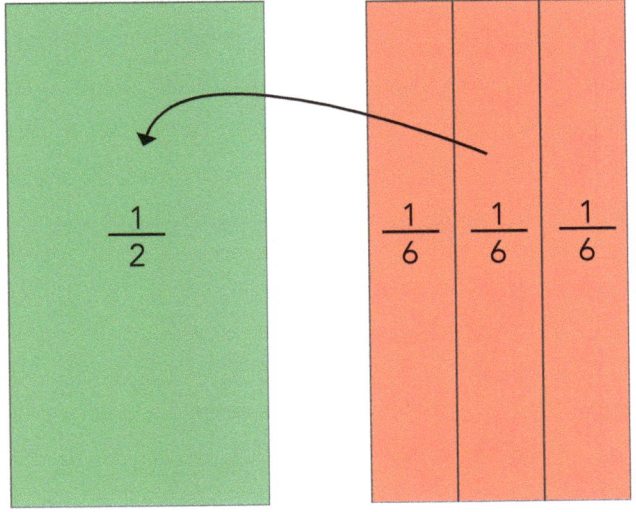

$$\frac{1}{2} \div \frac{1}{6} = 3$$

How many $\frac{1}{6}$ fit into $\frac{1}{2}$?

Perfect School Collection™

Copyright © 2023 by Lyle Lee Jenkins and Peggy McLean

All rights reserved. No part of this publication may be reproduced, distributed, or transmitted in any form or by any means, including photocopying, recording, or other electronic or mechanical methods, without the prior written permission of the publisher, LtoJ Press, except in the case of brief quotations embodied in critical reviews and certain other non-commercial uses permitted by copyright law.

To contact the authors regarding keynotes, workshops or bulk orders visit LtoJ.net/Contact

ISBN: 978-1-956457-77-3

Book Design & Graphics: Christy Courtright, Christy's Customs LLC
Quality Assurance Manager: Kelly Lippert
Publishing Consultant: Martha Bullen, Bullen Publishing Services
Distribution Coordinator: Maggie McLaughlin

Printed in the United States of America

The Perfect School Collection™

How to Create a Perfect School by Lyle Lee Jenkins
How to Create a Perfect Home School by Lyle Lee Jenkins and Kelly Hawkinson Lippert

Perfect School Collection™ Resources

How to Create Math Experts series by Peggy McLean and Lyle Lee Jenkins
How to Create Math Experts with Fluency Quizzes by Peggy McLean and Lyle Lee Jenkins
How to Create Math Experts with Math Standards Quizzes by Lyle Lee Jenkins, Peggy McLean, and Laura Hayes
How to Create a Math Foundation for Future Math Experts by Lyle Lee Jenkins
How to Create Language Experts with Literary Terms series by Codi Hrouda and Emma McInerney with Lyle Lee Jenkins
How to Create Bible Experts: Genesis to Revelation by Richard Douglas Junior Jenkins with Lyle Lee Jenkins

Young Readers

Bible Patterns for Young Readers series by Lyle Lee Jenkins
Aesop Patterns for Young Readers series by Lyle Lee Jenkins

Young Authors

Wordless Books for Young Authors series by Jim Chansler and Lyle Lee Jenkins

Special Project

All About Henry: Rich Widower of Savannah Valley by Lyle Lee Jenkins

CONTENTS

Purchasers of *How to Create Math Experts with Fraction Slices™* by Lyle Lee Jenkins and Peggy McLean may utilize the QR code provided at the end of the book to download worksheets from this book at no extra cost. This will ease the process of making copies for individual students. Both the print and downloaded copies are protected by copyright laws.

Introduction

LYLE LEE JENKINS AND PEGGY MCLEAN created a series of elementary math books to offer teachers proven resources for helping children master essential math concepts. Each book guides children to gain powerful lifelong math insights. Confidence builds more and more as children increase their math skills and knowledge from a young age. *How to Create Math Experts with Fraction Slices™* is true to its title. Adults and children are amazed at what they learn from this powerful collection of colorful transparent slices.

The Math Experts series subtitle, Constant Thrill from Success, does not mean immediate thrill or immediate success. When people are intrinsically motivated, they work hard, and the thrill comes from the learning. The aim is for students to be 100% engaged and love learning. The biggest thrill usually comes from a struggle over several days to finally solve a problem.

How to Create Math Experts with Fraction Slices™ is included within *The Perfect School Collection™* because it is an immense help in preserving intrinsic motivation. Lyle Lee Jenkins defines a perfect school as one in which the intrinsic motivation children bring with them to kindergarten is maintained for the next 12 years.

The metaphor of a tree with roots illustrates the process of children developing new skills. Images of trees rarely include the roots because they are hidden from view. However, we all know that if the roots die, it won't be long until the visible tree dies. John Hattie's "skill, will and thrill" learning model captures the thoughts behind the tree with roots. The visible tree is the math skill to be learned with Fraction Slices™. The invisible roots represent the will and the thrill maintaining students' natural love of learning. When students' natural love of learning (intrinsic motivation) is destroyed, it is not very long before the visible tree (skills) falters and dies. That is why math skills must be learned in such an exciting way that children's intrinsic motivation is maintained at a very high level!

Ask adults and high school students to estimate how many high school students are as excited about school learning as they once were as kindergartners. The research shows that 5 to 8% of students keep this love of learning for 13 years of K-12 education. We can do better. *The Perfect School Collection™* books will greatly increase this percentage.

Children can play with hammers, screw drivers, and levels, but adults do not call these objects toys. Children can also play with Fraction Slices™, but it would be a mistake to call them toys; they are tools just like rulers, compasses, and protractors. In fact, Fraction Slices™ are one of the most powerful tools ever invented to give children a solid understanding of equations with fractions.

The thrill of learning does not come from remembering rules and formulas often taught in math and phonics. It comes from children, with tools, figuring out solutions on their own.

As mentioned earlier, the problems in *How to Create Math Experts with Fraction Slices™* might not be solved instantly. When children are stumped and have no more energy for the task at hand, we suggest they move on to something else. We all know that solutions to adult problems often occur when not thinking directly about the problem. The solution can "pop into our heads" while in the shower, driving the car, or while we are on a walk or run. The same is true for children. While riding a bike, lying in bed, or sitting in the back seat of the car, children can have an "aha moment" and can hardly wait to get a hold of the Fraction Slices™ to see if their "aha" is correct. When it is, we call this thrilling success.

Thrill does not come from an adult placing a check mark by a problem that is incorrect. When an adult is looking over a student's work, the adult should place a "c" by correct answers and a simple dot by incorrect ones. The dot means *temporarily wrong*. When the children correct the mistake, the "c" covers up the dot, and all problems on the page have a "c." A paper with all "c's" can be proudly shared with parents and other important people in a child's life. Constant thrill from success will become your and your students' reality with *How to Create Math Experts with Fraction Slices™*.

Materials Needed:
Fraction Slices™
Available from Amazon

Getting Started

How to Create Math Experts with Fraction Slices™ was written for students to truly understand fraction operations with addition, subtraction, multiplication, and division prior to learning the short cuts. Historically, people figured out how fractions worked. Then, people developed short cuts that are labeled formulas. The problem with all short cuts is they almost always take more time in the long run. We do want students to learn formulas. However, formulas are taught after the deep understanding has taken place. Fraction Slices™ provide this deep understanding of foundational concepts along with the fraction learning from Pattern Blocks, GeoBoards, Tangrams, and GeoBlocks.

Many times the students will figure out the formulas for computation on their own and will not need to be taught them. We have heard students say, "There is a trick here; once we figure out the trick, we do not need the Fraction Slices™." This is ideal. However, it is okay to assist students in learning the formulas, but patience is required to not jump into formulas too soon. Let the children use the slices and actually learn much more than most adults know about fractions. It's magical.

PLEASE do not rush the movement from using the slices to only pencil and paper math. Children know that adults do not carry slices around in their purses and pockets and naturally strive to solve problems without them. The difference with a Fraction Slice™ foundation is the children are not trying to remember rules, but they have the pictures of their slices in their heads as they attempt to solve problems without any manipulatives in hand.

All problems and examples featured in *How to Create Math Experts with Fraction Slices™* are meant to be solved with the Fraction Slice™ Set. These powerful tools are used to create a foundational knowledge of what fractions are and how they interact through each operation (+, -, x, ÷). We know that the slices cannot be used for every fraction equation your child may encounter, but, working through the concepts provided within this workbook will equip your child to visualize what needs to happen for fraction equations they encounter in the future.

There is no order for the problems and explanations in *How To Create Math Experts with Fraction Slices™*. Start with division if you desire. Because books have page numbers it is assumed that students must complete every page before moving onto the next page in the book. Skip around to learn what looks interesting. Children will remember more if they cycle back to complete the pages they started earlier.

After students have completed the page, adults will correct it. Typically if an error occurs it is because the student thought they did not need the Fraction Slices™ to answer the question. The adult merely says, "Ask the slices what the correct answer is and let me know what you learned." You can tell the children that asking the slices for the answer is like asking the GPS for directions. Mom says, "I know the way; I do not need the GPS." The family gets lost and Mom opens up the GPS. The car is going in the wrong direction temporarily, not permanently. The same is true with mathematics.

Included with this book is a QR code to download a PDF of the worksheets in this book. This empowers your child to continue to practice and showcase continuous improvement in their educational journey.

On our website, www.LtoJ.net under Free Resources, you will also find an answer key for all worksheets.

MEET THE FRACTION SLICES™

This piece is called: ONE WHOLE

Write **1** when referencing this piece

How many $\frac{1}{2}$ slices cover one whole?

This symbol (÷) means divide, and this symbol (—) also means divide. So, $\frac{1}{2}$ means 1 divided by 2.

With Fraction Slices™ one whole slice has been divided into two equal parts.

$$\frac{1}{2} \quad + \quad \frac{1}{2} \quad = \quad \frac{2}{2} \quad = \quad \square$$

How many $\frac{1}{3}$ slices cover one whole?

One whole slice has been divided into three equal parts.

$$\frac{1}{3} \quad + \quad \frac{1}{3} \quad + \quad \frac{1}{3} \quad = \quad \frac{3}{3} \quad = \quad \boxed{}$$

How many $\frac{1}{4}$ slices cover one whole?

One whole slice has been divided into four equal parts.

$$\frac{1}{4} + \frac{1}{4} + \frac{1}{4} + \frac{1}{4} = \frac{4}{4} = \boxed{}$$

How many $\frac{1}{6}$ slices cover one whole?

One whole slice has been divided into six equal parts.

$$\frac{1}{6} + \frac{1}{6} + \frac{1}{6} + \frac{1}{6} + \frac{1}{6} + \frac{1}{6} = \frac{6}{6} = \boxed{}$$

How many $\frac{1}{8}$ slices cover one whole?

One whole slice has been divided into eight equal parts.

$$\frac{1}{8} + \frac{1}{8} + \frac{1}{8} + \frac{1}{8} + \frac{1}{8} + \frac{1}{8} + \frac{1}{8} + \frac{1}{8} = \frac{8}{8} = \boxed{}$$

How many $\frac{1}{12}$ slices cover one whole?

One whole has been divided into twelve equal parts.

$$\frac{1}{12}+\frac{1}{12}+\frac{1}{12}+\frac{1}{12}+\frac{1}{12}+\frac{1}{12}+\frac{1}{12}+\frac{1}{12}+\frac{1}{12}+\frac{1}{12}+\frac{1}{12}+\frac{1}{12}=\frac{12}{12}=\boxed{}$$

What color is each Fraction Slice™?

Keep this color key handy

1 whole is: _____

$\frac{1}{2}$ is: _____

$\frac{1}{3}$ is: _____

$\frac{1}{4}$ is: _____

$\frac{1}{6}$ is: _____

$\frac{1}{8}$ is: _____

$\frac{1}{12}$ is: _____

FRACTION IDENTIFICATION

How many $\dfrac{1}{2}$ slices cover the 1 whole piece? _____

How many $\dfrac{1}{3}$ slices cover the 1 whole piece? _____

How many $\dfrac{1}{4}$ slices cover the 1 whole piece? _____

How many $\dfrac{1}{6}$ slices cover the 1 whole piece? _____

How many $\dfrac{1}{8}$ slices cover the 1 whole piece? _____

How many $\dfrac{1}{12}$ slices cover the 1 whole piece?_____

EQUIVALENT FRACTIONS

Children know that there are many ways to communicate 4.

It could be:

2 + 2 =   or   8 - 4 =   or   2 x 2 =   or   12 ÷ 3 =

The same is true for fractions; ½ is the same as $^2/_4$, $^3/_6$, or $^{50}/_{100}$. The three fractions are all equivalent to ½. There is no limit to the number of equivalent fractions, but with Fraction Slices™, students will learn the equivalent fractions that can be shown using the slices. With the slices, for example, children will learn that ½ is equivalent to $^2/_4$, $^3/_6$, $^4/_8$, and $^6/_{12}$.

The problems are written as a pair of equivalent fractions with one of the 4 numerals missing.

For example:

$$\frac{1}{3} = \frac{?}{12}$$

Have students build the problem with their Fraction Slices™

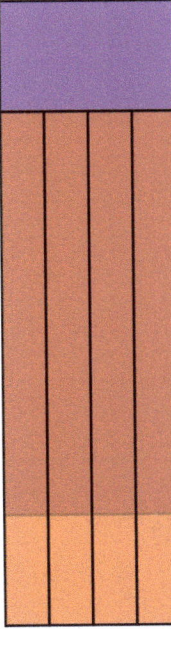

In this example, you can see that four $^1/_{12}$ pieces are exactly the same as one $^1/_3$.

$$\frac{1}{3} = \frac{4}{12}$$

TRY SOME EQUIVALENT FRACTIONS

Use Fraction Slices™ to complete each equation below.

$$1 = \frac{2}{2}$$

$$1 = \frac{\Box}{3}$$

$$1 = \frac{\Box}{4}$$

$$1 = \frac{\Box}{6}$$

$$1 = \frac{\Box}{8}$$

$$1 = \frac{\Box}{12}$$

TRY SOME MORE EQUIVALENT FRACTIONS

Use Fraction Slices™ to complete each equation below.

$$\frac{1}{2} = \frac{\boxed{}}{4}$$

$$\frac{1}{2} = \frac{\boxed{}}{6}$$

$$\frac{2}{2} = \frac{\boxed{}}{8}$$

$$\frac{1}{2} = \frac{\boxed{}}{8}$$

$$\frac{1}{2} = \frac{\boxed{}}{12}$$

$$\frac{2}{2} = \frac{\boxed{}}{3}$$

$$\frac{2}{2} = \frac{\boxed{}}{4}$$

$$\frac{2}{2} = \frac{\boxed{}}{12}$$

TRY EVEN MORE EQUIVALENT FRACTIONS

Use Fraction Slices™ to fill in the missing numerator.

$$\frac{1}{3} = \frac{\boxed{}}{6} \qquad\qquad \frac{1}{3} = \frac{\boxed{}}{12}$$

$$\frac{3}{3} = \frac{\boxed{}}{6}$$

$$\frac{2}{3} = \frac{\boxed{}}{6} \qquad\qquad \frac{2}{3} = \frac{\boxed{}}{12}$$

$$\frac{3}{3} = \frac{\boxed{}}{2}$$

$$\frac{3}{3} = \frac{\boxed{}}{6} \qquad\qquad \frac{3}{3} = \frac{\boxed{}}{12}$$

TRY SOME MORE EQUIVALENT FRACTIONS

Use Fraction Slices™ to fill in the missing numerator.

$$\frac{1}{4} = \frac{\Box}{8}$$

$$\frac{2}{4} = \frac{\Box}{8}$$

$$\frac{3}{4} = \frac{\Box}{8}$$

$$\frac{1}{4} = \frac{\Box}{12}$$

$$\frac{2}{4} = \frac{\Box}{12}$$

$$\frac{3}{4} = \frac{\Box}{12}$$

$$\frac{1}{6} = \frac{\Box}{12}$$

$$\frac{5}{6} = \frac{\Box}{12}$$

ADDITION
PARTS THAT EQUAL A WHOLE

With the Fraction Slices™, students will show many different ways to divide the one whole Fraction Slice™ into various fractions. As long as the chosen fraction slices fit exactly on the one whole piece, the students have shown another way to make one whole.

For example:

$$\frac{1}{3} + \frac{1}{6} + \frac{1}{4} + \frac{1}{8} + \frac{1}{8} = 1$$

As you can see below, these 5 slices cover the one whole exactly.

In addition to acquainting students with the Fraction Slices™, the purpose is for young children to see how parts of a whole are divided up very precisely.

ADDITION
PARTS THAT EQUAL ONE WHOLE

What fraction completes the square?

Write your answer in the equation below.

$$\frac{1}{2}$$

?

$$\frac{1}{4}$$

$$\frac{1}{2} \;+\; \frac{\boxed{}}{\boxed{}} \;+\; \frac{1}{4} \;=\; 1$$

ADDITION
PARTS THAT EQUAL ONE WHOLE

Label the missing fractions of the square.

Write your answer in the equation below.

$$\frac{1}{3} + \frac{1}{3} + \frac{\square}{\square} + \frac{\square}{\square} = 1$$

ADDITION
PARTS THAT EQUAL ONE WHOLE

What fractions complete the square?

Write your answer in the equation below.

?
$\frac{1}{12}$
$\frac{1}{4}$
?
?
$\frac{1}{12}$

$$\frac{\boxed{}}{\boxed{}} + \frac{1}{12} + \frac{1}{4} + \frac{\boxed{}}{\boxed{}} + \frac{\boxed{}}{\boxed{}} + \frac{1}{12} = 1$$

ADDITION
PARTS THAT EQUAL ONE WHOLE

Label the missing fractions of the square.

Write your answer in the equation below.

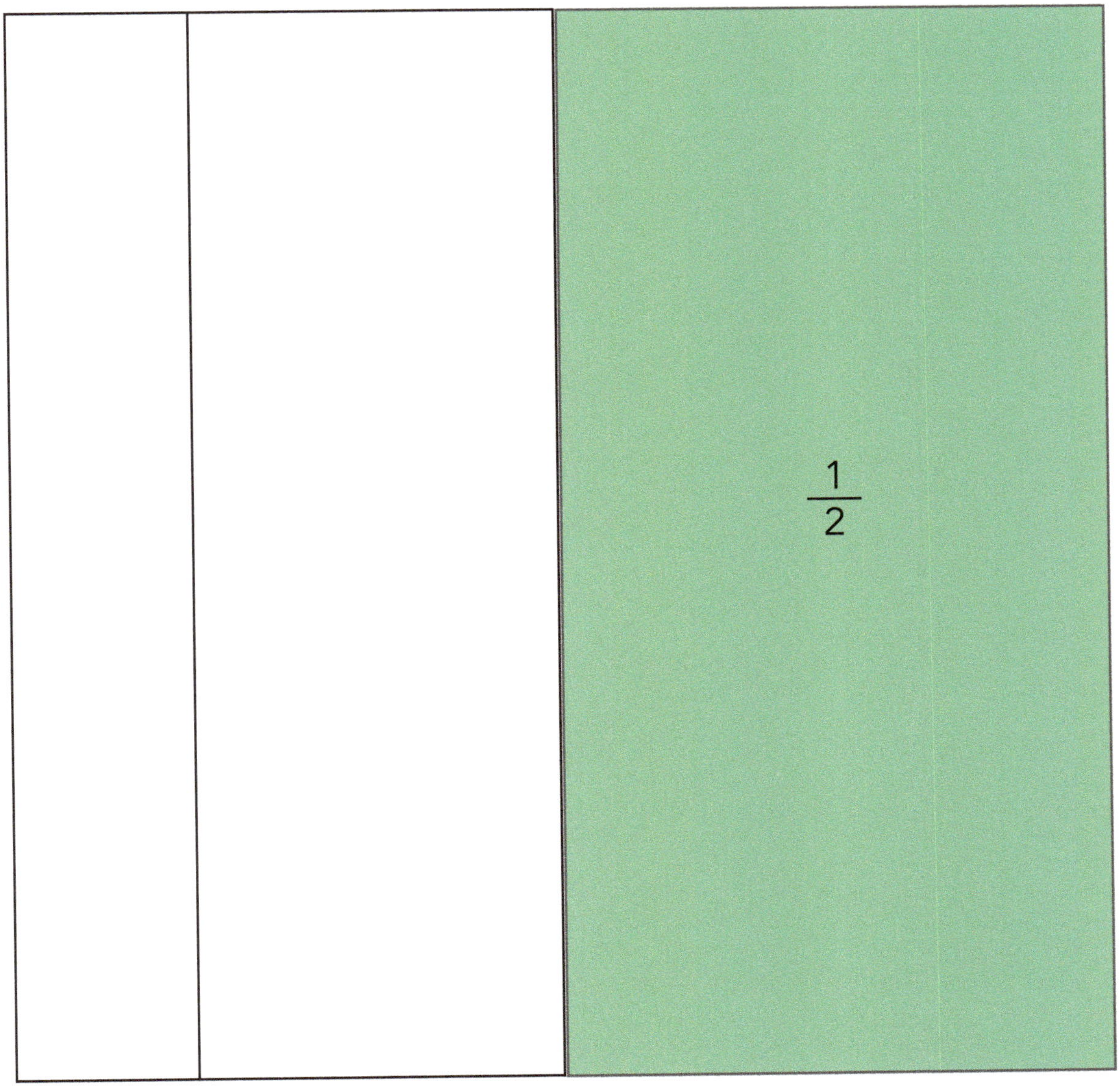

$$\frac{1}{2}$$

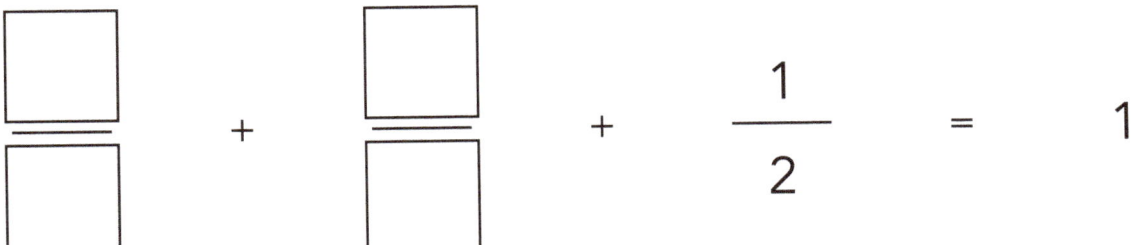

$$\frac{}{} + \frac{}{} + \frac{1}{2} = 1$$

Use the Fraction Slices™ to solve the problem below.

Solve for the fraction that represents the shaded part, and for the fraction that represents the non-shaded part.

Not shaded   +   Shaded   =   1

Use the Fraction Slices™ to solve the problem below.

Solve for the fraction that represents the shaded part, and for the fraction that represents the non-shaded part.

Not shaded $\quad$ + $\quad$ Shaded $\quad$ = $\quad$ 1

Use the Fraction Slices™ to solve the problem below.

Solve for the fraction that represents the shaded part, and for the fraction that represents the non-shaded part.

Shaded + Not shaded = 1

Time for a tricky one!

Solve for the fraction that represents the shaded parts, and for the fraction that represents the non-shaded parts.

Shaded + Not shaded + Not shaded + Shaded = 1

WHO KNEW THERE WERE SO MANY WAYS TO MAKE 1?

$$\frac{1}{2} + \frac{1}{2} = \underline{\qquad}$$

Build each equation using the correct slices laid together side by side. Pick one color of Fraction Slices™ that perfectly fits on top.

$$\frac{1}{3} + \frac{1}{3} + \frac{1}{3} = \underline{\qquad}$$

$$\frac{1}{4} + \frac{1}{4} + \frac{1}{4} + \frac{1}{4} = \underline{\qquad}$$

$$\frac{1}{6} + \frac{1}{6} + \frac{1}{6} + \frac{1}{6} + \frac{1}{6} + \frac{1}{6} = \underline{\qquad}$$

$$\frac{1}{8} + \frac{1}{8} + \frac{1}{8} + \frac{1}{8} + \frac{1}{8} + \frac{1}{8} + \frac{1}{8} + \frac{1}{8} = \underline{\qquad}$$

MORE WAYS TO MAKE 1

Build each equation using the correct slices laid together side by side. Pick one color of Fraction Slices™ that perfectly fits on top.

$$\frac{1}{2} + \frac{1}{2} = \underline{\hspace{1cm}}$$

$$\frac{1}{4} + \frac{1}{4} + \frac{1}{2} = \underline{\hspace{1cm}}$$

$$\frac{1}{6} + \frac{1}{6} + \frac{1}{6} + \frac{1}{2} = \underline{\hspace{1cm}}$$

$$\frac{1}{8} + \frac{1}{8} + \frac{1}{8} + \frac{1}{8} + \frac{1}{2} = \underline{\hspace{1cm}}$$

$$\frac{1}{12} + \frac{1}{12} + \frac{1}{12} + \frac{1}{12} + \frac{1}{12} + \frac{1}{12} + \frac{1}{2} = \underline{\hspace{1cm}}$$

FRACTION SLICE™ GAME

$$\frac{2}{6} \qquad \frac{1}{2} \qquad \frac{5}{8} \qquad \frac{1}{4} \qquad \frac{1}{3} \qquad \frac{3}{6} \qquad \frac{1}{8} \qquad \frac{9}{12}$$

$$\frac{2}{8} \qquad \frac{1}{2} \qquad \frac{1}{4} \qquad \frac{1}{12} \qquad \frac{2}{4} \qquad \frac{2}{12} \qquad \frac{1}{6} \qquad \frac{2}{3}$$

- DIRECTIONS -

1. Flip a coin to decide who goes first.

2. The first person chooses a fraction and draws a rectangle around the fraction.

   Example: $\boxed{\dfrac{2}{3}}$

3. The second person chooses a fraction and draws a circle around the fraction.

   Example: $\left(\dfrac{9}{12}\right)$

4. Continue until each player has chosen 8 fractions.

5. Collect the Fraction Slices™ that match the fractions you have chosen. The winner is the person whose fractions add up to be the largest number.

6. Play again with the other person going first.

COMPARING FRACTIONS

Children learn the order for numerals, for instance, that 17 is more than 13. Then along come fractions. Adults might trick a child by asking, "Do you want a ¹/₁₂ of the candy bar or a ⅓ of the bar?" Of course, young children will often ask for the ¹/₁₂ of the candy bar assuming it is larger than the ⅓. What a disappointing way to learn about smaller and larger fractions. When comparing fractions using Fraction Slices™, children will physically pick up the slices to confirm.

For example:

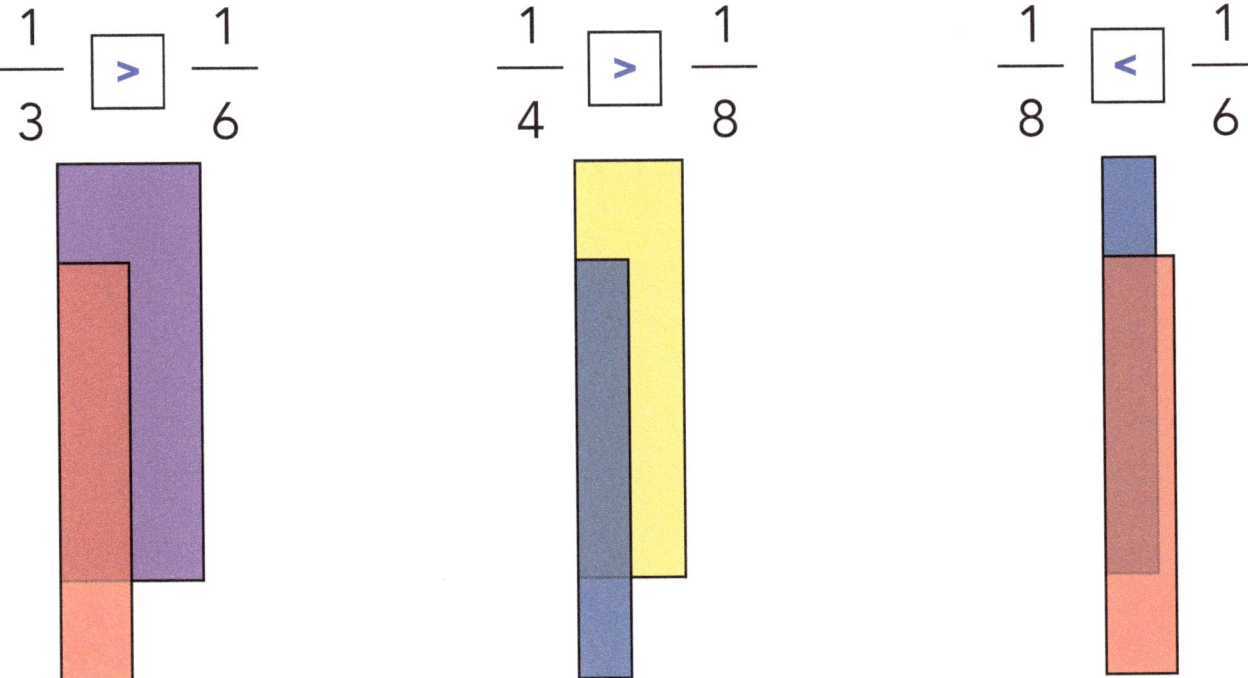

Students are to place an =, < or > between the two fractions. Adults can explain the < and > symbols in one of two ways. One explanation is to always point to the smaller numeral. Thus with the problem ½ and ¼ the symbol points to the smaller numeral: ½ > ¼. The other way to explain the < and > symbols is to think of an alligator eating the larger numeral. Thus with the problem comparing ½ and ¾ the student will write ½ < ¾ because the alligator is eating the larger numeral ¾.

TRY COMPARING FRACTIONS

Place greater than **>** or less than **<** between each pair.

$\frac{1}{2}$ $\boxed{<}$ 1

$\frac{1}{3}$ $\boxed{\phantom{<}}$ 1

$\frac{1}{2}$ $\boxed{\phantom{<}}$ $\frac{1}{3}$

$\frac{1}{3}$ $\boxed{\phantom{<}}$ $\frac{1}{2}$

$\frac{1}{2}$ $\boxed{\phantom{<}}$ $\frac{1}{4}$

$\frac{1}{3}$ $\boxed{\phantom{<}}$ $\frac{1}{4}$

$\frac{1}{3}$ $\boxed{\phantom{<}}$ $\frac{1}{6}$

$\frac{1}{2}$ $\boxed{\phantom{<}}$ $\frac{1}{6}$

$\frac{1}{2}$ $\boxed{\phantom{<}}$ $\frac{1}{8}$

$\frac{1}{3}$ $\boxed{\phantom{<}}$ $\frac{1}{8}$

TRY MORE COMPARING FRACTIONS

Place greater than **>** or less than **<** between each pair.

$\frac{1}{4}$ ☐ 1

$\frac{1}{6}$ ☐ 1

$\frac{1}{4}$ ☐ $\frac{1}{2}$

$\frac{1}{6}$ ☐ $\frac{1}{2}$

$\frac{1}{4}$ ☐ $\frac{1}{3}$

$\frac{1}{6}$ ☐ $\frac{1}{3}$

$\frac{1}{4}$ ☐ $\frac{1}{6}$

$\frac{1}{6}$ ☐ $\frac{1}{4}$

$\frac{1}{4}$ ☐ $\frac{1}{8}$

$\frac{1}{6}$ ☐ $\frac{1}{8}$

TRY SOME MORE COMPARING FRACTIONS

Place greater than **>** or less than **<** between each pair.

$\frac{1}{8}$ ☐ 1　　　　　　　　$\frac{1}{12}$ ☐ 1

$\frac{1}{8}$ ☐ $\frac{1}{2}$　　　　　　$\frac{1}{12}$ ☐ $\frac{1}{2}$

$\frac{1}{8}$ ☐ $\frac{1}{3}$　　　　　　$\frac{1}{12}$ ☐ $\frac{1}{3}$

$\frac{1}{8}$ ☐ $\frac{1}{4}$　　　　　　$\frac{1}{12}$ ☐ $\frac{1}{4}$

$\frac{1}{8}$ ☐ $\frac{1}{6}$　　　　　　$\frac{1}{12}$ ☐ $\frac{1}{6}$

TRY EVEN MORE COMPARING FRACTIONS

Place greater than **>**, less than **<**, or equal **=** between each pair.

$\dfrac{1}{6}$ ☐ $\dfrac{1}{3}$ $\dfrac{1}{4}$ ☐ $\dfrac{2}{8}$

$\dfrac{1}{2}$ ☐ $\dfrac{1}{4}$ $\dfrac{1}{3}$ ☐ $\dfrac{1}{2}$

$\dfrac{1}{2}$ ☐ $\dfrac{2}{4}$ $\dfrac{2}{3}$ ☐ $\dfrac{1}{2}$

$\dfrac{1}{2}$ ☐ $\dfrac{3}{4}$ $\dfrac{3}{3}$ ☐ $\dfrac{2}{2}$

$\dfrac{2}{6}$ ☐ $\dfrac{1}{3}$ $\dfrac{1}{4}$ ☐ $\dfrac{3}{8}$

MORE
COMPARING FRACTIONS

Place greater than **>**, less than **<**, or equal **=** between each pair.

$\dfrac{2}{6}$ ☐ $\dfrac{2}{3}$ $\dfrac{1}{4}$ ☐ $\dfrac{4}{8}$

$\dfrac{3}{6}$ ☐ $\dfrac{1}{2}$ $\dfrac{3}{6}$ ☐ $\dfrac{3}{4}$

$\dfrac{3}{6}$ ☐ $\dfrac{2}{4}$ $\dfrac{4}{12}$ ☐ $\dfrac{1}{3}$

$\dfrac{4}{12}$ ☐ $\dfrac{2}{3}$ $\dfrac{7}{12}$ ☐ $\dfrac{4}{6}$

$\dfrac{5}{12}$ ☐ $\dfrac{1}{3}$ $\dfrac{7}{12}$ ☐ $\dfrac{1}{2}$

EVEN MORE COMPARING FRACTIONS

Place greater than >, less than <, or equal = between each pair.

$\frac{4}{8}$ ☐ $\frac{1}{2}$ $\frac{1}{3}$ ☐ $\frac{2}{6}$

$\frac{5}{8}$ ☐ $\frac{1}{2}$ $\frac{5}{8}$ ☐ $\frac{3}{4}$

$\frac{3}{6}$ ☐ $\frac{1}{2}$ $\frac{1}{3}$ ☐ $\frac{4}{12}$

$\frac{6}{8}$ ☐ $\frac{3}{4}$ $\frac{7}{8}$ ☐ $\frac{3}{4}$

$\frac{5}{8}$ ☐ $\frac{1}{2}$ $\frac{7}{12}$ ☐ $\frac{2}{3}$

GREATER THAN - LESS THAN

Put these fractions in order from smallest to largest.

$\frac{1}{2}$, $\frac{1}{3}$, $\frac{2}{3}$ $\frac{1}{3}$ < $\frac{1}{2}$ < $\boxed{} \over \boxed{}$

SMALLEST ⟶ LARGEST

$\frac{1}{3}$, $\frac{8}{12}$, $\frac{3}{6}$ $\frac{\boxed{}}{\boxed{}}$ < $\frac{\boxed{}}{\boxed{}}$ < $\frac{\boxed{}}{\boxed{}}$

$\frac{1}{2}$, $\frac{1}{4}$, $\frac{4}{12}$, $\frac{5}{8}$ $\frac{\boxed{}}{\boxed{}}$ < $\frac{\boxed{}}{\boxed{}}$ < $\frac{\boxed{}}{\boxed{}}$ < $\frac{\boxed{}}{\boxed{}}$

$\frac{1}{2}$, $\frac{2}{3}$, $\frac{7}{12}$, $\frac{7}{8}$ $\frac{\boxed{}}{\boxed{}}$ < $\frac{\boxed{}}{\boxed{}}$ < $\frac{\boxed{}}{\boxed{}}$ < $\frac{\boxed{}}{\boxed{}}$

$\frac{1}{2}$, $\frac{3}{4}$, $\frac{1}{4}$, $\frac{11}{12}$ $\frac{\boxed{}}{\boxed{}}$ < $\frac{\boxed{}}{\boxed{}}$ < $\frac{\boxed{}}{\boxed{}}$ < $\frac{\boxed{}}{\boxed{}}$

NUMBER LINE COMPARISON

People are often asked to visualize fractions on a number line. Rulers and wrenches are examples. Place these wrench sizes or ruler lengths in order from smallest to largest; for example: ⅜", ¼", ¾", ½", ⅝". With number line comparison and fraction slices, students can connect the slices with the number line and visually see how their sizes compare.

Put each fraction on the number line.
Use the top edge ∏ of the Fraction Slice™ to measure.

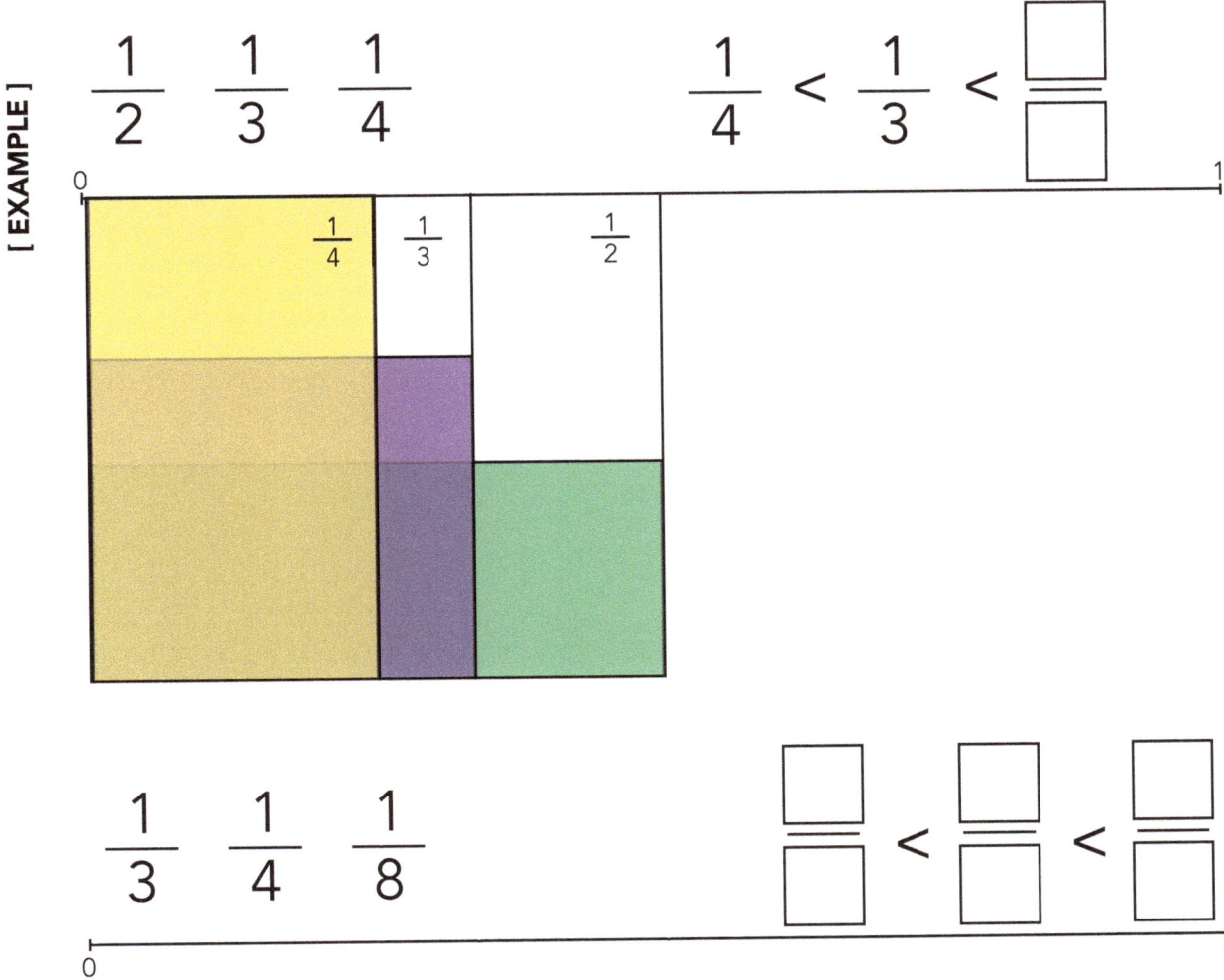

$$\frac{1}{2} \quad \frac{1}{3} \quad \frac{1}{4}$$

$$\frac{1}{4} < \frac{1}{3} < \frac{\Box}{\Box}$$

$$\frac{1}{3} \quad \frac{1}{4} \quad \frac{1}{8}$$

$$\frac{\Box}{\Box} < \frac{\Box}{\Box} < \frac{\Box}{\Box}$$

NUMBER LINE COMPARISON

Put each fraction on the number line.
Use the top edge ∏ of the Fraction Slice™ to measure.

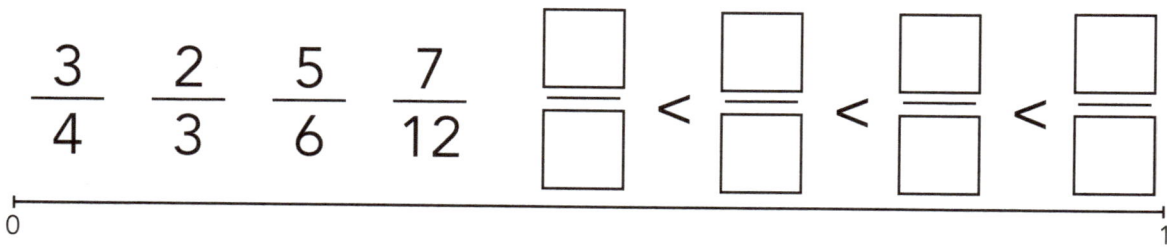

$$\frac{3}{4} \quad \frac{2}{3} \quad \frac{5}{6} \quad \frac{7}{12}$$

$$\frac{\square}{\square} < \frac{\square}{\square} < \frac{\square}{\square} < \frac{\square}{\square}$$

0 ——————————————————— 1

$$\frac{5}{8} \quad \frac{1}{2} \quad \frac{1}{6} \quad \frac{5}{12}$$

$$\frac{\square}{\square} < \frac{\square}{\square} < \frac{\square}{\square} < \frac{\square}{\square}$$

0 ——————————————————— 1

SPLICING FRACTIONS (ADDITION)

Adding with whole numbers and with fractions is the same concept - putting items together and writing down the total. We can combine 6 plus 3 and similarly we can solve ⅙ + ⅓. With the Fraction Slices™ the fraction problem is as simple as the whole number problem.

Students are instructed to:

1. Pick up the ⅙ slice and the ⅓ slice.

2. Place the two slices adjacent to each other.

3. Cover the two slices with other slices. Use only one color to cover the original pieces.

$$\frac{1}{3} + \frac{1}{6} =$$

4. ½ will be the most common answer, but ²⁄₄ and ³⁄₆ are also correct answers.

Fraction Slices™ eliminate the need to find the common denominator and to reduce to lowest terms. These short cuts will be learned after the foundational understanding is developed. After sufficient practice with Fraction Slices™, students will naturally solve some problems with their minds without the use of slices. Fractions should be a source of joy for students as they proceed with confidence.

Don't teach common denominator formula yet. Children should understand the concept prior to formulas.

TRY SPLICING FRACTIONS

Build each fraction. Put them together side by side. Pick one color of Fraction Slices™ that perfectly covers both fractions.

$\dfrac{1}{3} + \dfrac{1}{6} = \dfrac{\square}{\square}$
$\qquad$
$\dfrac{1}{4} + \dfrac{1}{2} = \dfrac{\square}{\square}$
$\qquad$
$\dfrac{3}{12} + \dfrac{1}{4} = \dfrac{\square}{\square}$

$\dfrac{1}{2} + \dfrac{1}{4} = \dfrac{\square}{\square}$
$\qquad$
$\dfrac{5}{8} + \dfrac{3}{8} = \dfrac{\square}{\square}$
$\qquad$
$\dfrac{4}{12} + \dfrac{1}{4} = \dfrac{\square}{\square}$

$\dfrac{1}{3} + \dfrac{2}{3} = \dfrac{\square}{\square}$
$\qquad$
$\dfrac{3}{8} + \dfrac{1}{8} = \dfrac{\square}{\square}$
$\qquad$
$\dfrac{5}{12} + \dfrac{1}{4} = \dfrac{\square}{\square}$

$\dfrac{1}{4} + \dfrac{1}{4} = \dfrac{\square}{\square}$
$\qquad$
$\dfrac{1}{8} + \dfrac{5}{8} = \dfrac{\square}{\square}$
$\qquad$
$\dfrac{6}{12} + \dfrac{1}{4} = \dfrac{\square}{\square}$

TRY SOME MORE SPLICING FRACTIONS

Build each fraction. Put them together side by side. Pick one color of Fraction Slices™ that perfectly covers both fractions.

$\dfrac{7}{12} + \dfrac{1}{4} = \dfrac{\boxed{}}{\boxed{}}$

$\dfrac{3}{8} + \dfrac{1}{4} = \dfrac{\boxed{}}{\boxed{}}$

$\dfrac{4}{8} + \dfrac{1}{3} = \dfrac{\boxed{}}{\boxed{}}$

$\dfrac{8}{12} + \dfrac{1}{4} = \dfrac{\boxed{}}{\boxed{}}$

$\dfrac{1}{12} + \dfrac{3}{4} = \dfrac{\boxed{}}{\boxed{}}$

$\dfrac{1}{8} + \dfrac{3}{8} = \dfrac{\boxed{}}{\boxed{}}$

$\dfrac{9}{12} + \dfrac{1}{4} = \dfrac{\boxed{}}{\boxed{}}$

$\dfrac{2}{12} + \dfrac{5}{6} = \dfrac{\boxed{}}{\boxed{}}$

$\dfrac{1}{6} + \dfrac{4}{8} = \dfrac{\boxed{}}{\boxed{}}$

$\dfrac{1}{4} + \dfrac{3}{4} = \dfrac{\boxed{}}{\boxed{}}$

$\dfrac{3}{4} + \dfrac{1}{8} = \dfrac{\boxed{}}{\boxed{}}$

$\dfrac{1}{2} + \dfrac{2}{6} = \dfrac{\boxed{}}{\boxed{}}$

TRY EVEN MORE SPLICING FRACTIONS

$$\frac{1}{6} + \frac{1}{6} = \frac{\boxed{}}{\boxed{}}$$

$$\frac{1}{4} + \frac{1}{4} = \frac{\boxed{}}{\boxed{}}$$

$$\frac{1}{3} + \frac{1}{3} = \frac{\boxed{}}{\boxed{}}$$

$$\frac{1}{3} + \frac{1}{6} = \frac{\boxed{}}{\boxed{}}$$

$$\frac{1}{6} + \frac{1}{3} = \frac{\boxed{}}{\boxed{}}$$

$$\frac{3}{8} + \frac{1}{4} = \frac{\boxed{}}{\boxed{}}$$

$$\frac{2}{8} + \frac{1}{4} = \frac{\boxed{}}{\boxed{}}$$

$$\frac{1}{2} + \frac{4}{8} = \frac{\boxed{}}{\boxed{}}$$

$$\frac{1}{2} + \frac{1}{3} = \frac{\boxed{}}{\boxed{}}$$

A CONCISE COMPARISON
(SUBTRACTION)

As explained in *How to Create Math Experts with Base Ten Blocks*, there are two concepts for subtraction. They are take-away and comparison. Sometimes we are asked to remove a number and the answer is how much is left. Take-away subtraction is when you remove a number and the answer is how much is left. This is the most common use of subtraction. Comparison subtraction is when you are asked how much larger one number is than another number. There is no taking away. The Fraction Slices™ utilize comparison to obtain the answer.

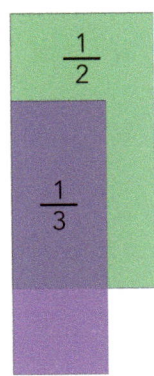

For example, lets take ½ - ⅓.

1. Pick up the ½ slice and place the ⅓ slice on top of it.

2. The question is asking how much larger is the ½ slice than the ⅓ slice.

3. The answer has to be one color of slices. The two possible correct answers with the slices are ⅙ or ²/₁₂.

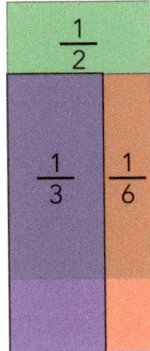 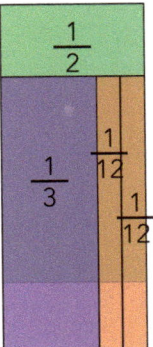

Children's transition from using the slices to being able to visualize the answers without the slices is exciting. Instead of students being bogged down with having to learn how to calculate common denominators and then reduce to lowest terms (and simultaneously being frustrated) they will happily have fraction concepts and computation happening in their minds.

SUBTRACTION BY COMPARISON WITH FRACTION SLICES™

Build the first fraction, then put the second fraction on top.
The fraction piece(s) that fit in the uncovered space is the answer.

$$\frac{3}{4} - \frac{1}{2} = \frac{\square}{\square}$$

$$\frac{9}{12} - \frac{1}{2} = \frac{\square}{\square}$$

$$\frac{5}{6} - \frac{1}{3} = \frac{\square}{\square}$$

$$\frac{7}{12} - \frac{1}{4} = \frac{\square}{\square}$$

$$\frac{5}{8} - \frac{3}{8} = \frac{\square}{\square}$$

$$\frac{3}{4} - \frac{3}{8} = \frac{\square}{\square}$$

$$\frac{1}{4} - \frac{1}{6} = \frac{\square}{\square}$$

$$\frac{11}{12} - \frac{5}{6} = \frac{\square}{\square}$$

MORE SUBTRACTION
BY COMPARISON

Build the first fraction, then put the second fraction on top.
The fraction piece(s) that fit in the uncovered space is the answer.

$$\frac{5}{8} - \frac{1}{4} = \frac{\Box}{\Box}$$

$$1 - \frac{1}{4} = \frac{\Box}{\Box}$$

$$\frac{3}{12} - \frac{1}{4} = \frac{\Box}{\Box}$$

$$\frac{6}{12} - \frac{1}{4} = \frac{\Box}{\Box}$$

$$\frac{4}{12} - \frac{1}{4} = \frac{\Box}{\Box}$$

$$\frac{9}{12} - \frac{1}{4} = \frac{\Box}{\Box}$$

$$\frac{5}{12} - \frac{1}{4} = \frac{\Box}{\Box}$$

$$\frac{8}{12} - \frac{1}{4} = \frac{\Box}{\Box}$$

EVEN MORE SUBTRACTION BY COMPARISON

Build the first fraction, then put the second fraction on top.
The fraction piece(s) that fit in the uncovered space is the answer.

$$\frac{1}{3} - \frac{2}{12} = \frac{\square}{\square}$$

$$\frac{1}{2} - \frac{3}{12} = \frac{\square}{\square}$$

$$\frac{1}{2} - \frac{2}{12} = \frac{\square}{\square}$$

$$\frac{1}{2} - \frac{4}{12} = \frac{\square}{\square}$$

$$\frac{2}{3} - \frac{1}{3} = \frac{\square}{\square}$$

$$\frac{5}{8} - \frac{1}{4} = \frac{\square}{\square}$$

$$\frac{10}{12} - \frac{1}{4} = \frac{\square}{\square}$$

$$\frac{9}{12} - \frac{2}{8} = \frac{\square}{\square}$$

LET'S DO SOME
MORE SUBTRACTION

Build the first fraction, then put the second fraction on top.
The fraction piece(s) that fit in the uncovered space is the answer.

$$\frac{1}{3} - \frac{1}{3} = \frac{\square}{\square}$$

$$\frac{1}{3} - \frac{1}{6} = \frac{\square}{\square}$$

$$\frac{1}{2} - \frac{1}{6} = \frac{\square}{\square}$$

$$\frac{1}{2} - \frac{1}{4} = \frac{\square}{\square}$$

$$\frac{1}{4} - \frac{1}{4} = \frac{\square}{\square}$$

$$\frac{3}{8} - \frac{2}{8} = \frac{\square}{\square}$$

$$\frac{3}{8} - \frac{1}{8} = \frac{\square}{\square}$$

$$\frac{2}{4} - \frac{1}{4} = \frac{\square}{\square}$$

BE PRECISE
(BEGINNING DIVISION)

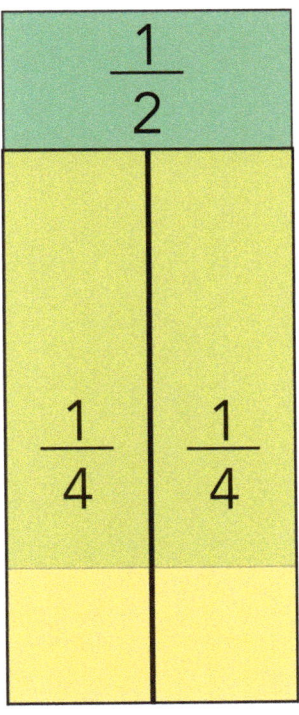

In one school district all grade six students took a common math assessment. The two division of fraction questions were ½ ÷ ¼ and ⅕ ÷ ⅕. Ninety percent of the students missed both questions. Why? They were all taught the short cut (formula) and didn't understand what the division of fraction problems were asking. The questions are asking (1) How many ¼'s can fit into ½? and (2) How many ⅕'s can fit into ⅕? The simple answers to these questions are 2 (because two ¼'s fit into ½) and 1 (because ⅕ can fit into another ⅕ one time).

Fraction Slices™ solve this problem. With the use of Fraction Slices™, students will be able to understand that you don't need a formula to solve many division of fraction questions. Later in their education they will learn two formulas for dividing fractions. It is important that they learn the why and how before formulas are introduced.

For example, lets solve ½ ÷ ⅛:

1. Pick up the slices needed for the problem. For our example, you will need one ½ slice and several of the ⅛'s slices. (remember the simple question: "How many of the ⅛ slices fit into the ½ slice?").

2. Place the ½ slice down and fill it with ⅛ slices, ensure they are a perfect fit.

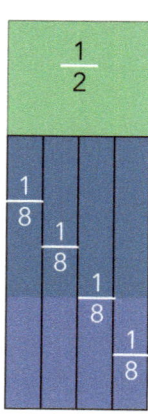

The answer is 4, because 4 of the ⅛ slices fit perfectly into the ½ slice. Something to note: do not expect to see the ⌐ bracket anywhere else in fraction work books. The reason for the bracket is to help children transition from division with whole numbers to division with fractions. In the beginning children sometimes stumble over ½ ÷ ¼. They do not know this means how many ¼'s are in ½. The children are more used to the bracket, so seeing ¼ ⟌½ helps them see the question, "how many ¼'s are in ½?"

BEGINNING DIVISION
WITH FRACTION SLICES™

$1 \div \dfrac{1}{8} = \boxed{}$

$1 \div \dfrac{1}{12} = \boxed{}$

$\dfrac{1}{8} \overline{\smash{)}\dfrac{1}{8}}$ $\boxed{}$

$\dfrac{1}{6} \overline{\smash{)}\dfrac{1}{3}}$ $\boxed{}$

$1 \div \dfrac{1}{6} = \boxed{}$

$\dfrac{1}{4} \div \dfrac{1}{8} = \boxed{}$

$\dfrac{1}{8} \overline{\smash{)}\dfrac{2}{4}}$ $\boxed{}$

$\dfrac{3}{12} \overline{\smash{)}\dfrac{2}{8}}$ $\boxed{}$

TRY SOME BEGINNING DIVISION WITH FRACTION SLICES™

$$\frac{1}{3} \div \frac{1}{6} = \boxed{}$$

$$\frac{2}{8} \div \frac{1}{4} = \boxed{}$$

$$\frac{1}{4} \div \frac{1}{8} = \boxed{}$$

$$\frac{3}{4} \div \frac{3}{8} = \boxed{}$$

$$\frac{1}{3} \div \frac{1}{12} = \boxed{}$$

$$\frac{5}{6} \div \frac{5}{12} = \boxed{}$$

$$\frac{1}{6} \div \frac{1}{12} = \boxed{}$$

$$\frac{2}{3} \div \frac{2}{6} = \boxed{}$$

TRY SOME MORE BEGINNING DIVISION WITH FRACTION SLICES™

$$\frac{6}{12} \div \frac{1}{4} = \boxed{}$$

$$\frac{4}{6} \div \frac{8}{12} = \boxed{}$$

$$\frac{4}{6} \div \frac{1}{3} = \boxed{}$$

$$\frac{1}{2} \div \frac{1}{12} = \boxed{}$$

$$\frac{6}{12} \div \frac{1}{8} = \boxed{}$$

$$\frac{1}{2} \div \frac{1}{4} = \boxed{}$$

GIVE THESE DIVISION PROBLEMS A TRY

$$\frac{1}{3} \div \frac{1}{12} = \boxed{}$$

$$\frac{3}{4} \div \frac{1}{8} = \boxed{}$$

$$\frac{1}{8} \overline{\smash{)}\,\frac{4}{4}}$$

$$\frac{1}{4} \overline{\smash{)}\,\frac{6}{8}}$$

$$\frac{3}{8} \div \frac{1}{8} = \boxed{}$$

$$\frac{2}{3} \div \frac{1}{6} = \boxed{}$$

$$\frac{1}{12} \overline{\smash{)}\,\frac{2}{3}}$$

$$\frac{1}{3} \overline{\smash{)}\,1}$$

EVEN MORE DIVISION
PROBLEMS TO TRY

$\frac{6}{8} \div \frac{1}{4} = \boxed{}$

$\frac{2}{12} \overline{)\frac{5}{6}}$ with $\boxed{}$ above

$\frac{1}{2} \div \frac{6}{12} = \boxed{}$

$\frac{1}{2} \overline{)\frac{1}{2}}$ with $\boxed{}$ above

$\frac{10}{12} \div \frac{1}{6} = \boxed{}$

$\frac{2}{8} \overline{)\frac{1}{2}}$ with $\boxed{}$ above

THE COMMON DENOMINATOR "TRICK"

In schools, almost always division of fractions is taught with the formula: invert the divisor and multiply, which is hard for children to remember. The formula is useful for problems like $3/13 \div 15/17$. With Fraction Slices™ the directions are to use one color tile for the answer which is the introductory way of arriving at a common denominator. Some may wonder why common denominators are left out of fraction division. When two fractions have the same denominator, the denominator is useless. $3/12 \div 7/12$ is $3/7$, the denominator is not needed. Thus $3/4 \div 7/8$ can be changed to $6/8 \div 7/8$, the answer is simply $6/7$; the denominator is not needed to solve the problem. There will be some answers that are improper fractions. Leave them as improper fractions. Let children have the thrill of discovering for themselves that improper fractions can be made into mixed numerals.

$$\frac{1}{2} \div \frac{1}{2} = \frac{\boxed{1}}{\boxed{1}} \qquad \frac{3}{4} \div \frac{1}{4} = \frac{\boxed{3}}{\boxed{1}} \qquad \frac{5}{8} \div \frac{1}{8} = \frac{\boxed{5}}{\boxed{1}}$$

$$\frac{2}{3} \div \frac{1}{3} = \frac{\boxed{}}{\boxed{}} \qquad \frac{7}{8} \div \frac{1}{8} = \frac{\boxed{}}{\boxed{}} \qquad \frac{6}{12} \div \frac{2}{12} = \frac{\boxed{}}{\boxed{}}$$

$$\frac{1}{8} \div \frac{1}{8} = \frac{\boxed{}}{\boxed{}} \qquad \frac{7}{8} \div \frac{1}{8} = \frac{\boxed{}}{\boxed{}} \qquad \frac{9}{12} \div \frac{3}{12} = \frac{\boxed{}}{\boxed{}}$$

$$\frac{6}{8} \div \frac{1}{8} = \frac{\boxed{}}{\boxed{}} \qquad \frac{5}{6} \div \frac{1}{6} = \frac{\boxed{}}{\boxed{}} \qquad \frac{1}{6} \div \frac{5}{6} = \frac{\boxed{}}{\boxed{}}$$

THE COMMON DENOMINATOR "TRICK"

$$\frac{3}{8} \div \frac{1}{8} = \frac{\Box}{\Box}$$

$$\frac{10}{12} \div \frac{2}{12} = \frac{\Box}{\Box}$$

$$\frac{4}{8} \div \frac{1}{8} = \frac{\Box}{\Box}$$

$$\frac{6}{8} \div \frac{3}{8} = \frac{\Box}{\Box}$$

$$\frac{4}{75} \div \frac{2}{75} = \frac{\Box}{\Box}$$

$$\frac{80}{712} \div \frac{10}{712} = \frac{\Box}{\Box}$$

$$\frac{6}{1043} \div \frac{2}{1043} = \frac{\Box}{\Box}$$

$$\frac{10}{613} \div \frac{5}{613} = \frac{\Box}{\Box}$$

DICE THEM UP!
(BEGINNING MULTIPLICATION)

The problem with fraction multiplication is very common: the formula to multiply numerators by numerators and denominators by denominators is so simple to teach. Students obtain the correct answer with no clue what it means. Most students never know the reason why the answer is a smaller number when they multiply fractions. They are used to multiplying 2 x 2 and the answer 4 is larger. However, when they multiply ½ x ½ and receive an answer of ¼, they are surprised about the answer being smaller. From the very beginning of using Fraction Slices™ for multiplication, students will learn why the answers produce a smaller number.

Lets work together and solve ⅔ x ²/₄:

The first step with solving multiplication of fraction problems is to find the denominator on the bottom. The second step is to find the numerator on the top. For our example, you will pick up all of the ⅓ pieces and all of the ¼ pieces. Take the first set of slices and make a perfect square, then take the second set of slices and stack them on top of the first set going the opposite direction.

If you count how many small rectangles there are in total you will have your denominator. In our example, there are 12 small rectangles, so we know that 12 is the denominator of our answer. For any fraction multiplication problem featuring ⅓'s and ¼'s 12 will be the denominator.

$$\frac{2}{3} \times \frac{2}{4} = \frac{\square}{12}$$

1	2	3
4	5	6
7	8	9
10	11	12

The second step is to determine the numerator that goes on top of the denominator at the bottom. Cross over the ends of the two of the ⅓'s and two of the ¼'s. Count the number of small rectangles, made by overlapping pieces. In our example, there are 4 small rectangles created when you overlap ⅔ and 2/4. Each of the small rectangles are 1/12 of the whole piece. Thus the answer the student writes on their paper is ⅔ x 2/4 = 4/12 because ⅔ x 2/4 is 4/12 of the whole Fraction Slice™.

1	2
3	4

$$\frac{2}{3} \times \frac{2}{4} = \frac{4}{12}$$

The first page of multiplication problems uses only ⅓ and ¼ slices so students can practice the two steps above. The remaining pages require students to pick up different slices along the way.

LET'S PRACTICE FINDING NUMERATORS AND DENOMINATORS

$\dfrac{1}{3} \times \dfrac{1}{4} = \dfrac{\square}{\square}$

$\dfrac{1}{3} \times \dfrac{3}{4} = \dfrac{\square}{\square}$

$\dfrac{2}{3} \times \dfrac{1}{4} = \dfrac{\square}{\square}$

$\dfrac{2}{3} \times \dfrac{3}{4} = \dfrac{\square}{\square}$

$\dfrac{3}{3} \times \dfrac{1}{4} = \dfrac{\square}{\square}$

$\dfrac{3}{3} \times \dfrac{3}{4} = \dfrac{\square}{\square}$

$\dfrac{1}{3} \times \dfrac{2}{4} = \dfrac{\square}{\square}$

$\dfrac{1}{3} \times \dfrac{4}{4} = \dfrac{\square}{\square}$

$\dfrac{2}{3} \times \dfrac{2}{4} = \dfrac{\square}{\square}$

$\dfrac{2}{3} \times \dfrac{4}{4} = \dfrac{\square}{\square}$

$\dfrac{3}{3} \times \dfrac{2}{4} = \dfrac{\square}{\square}$

$\dfrac{3}{3} \times \dfrac{4}{4} = \dfrac{\square}{\square}$

TRY SOME MULTIPLICATION

Use Fraction Slices™ to solve the equations below.

$$\frac{1}{2} \times \frac{2}{3} = \frac{\Box}{\Box}$$

$$\frac{1}{2} \times \frac{2}{6} = \frac{\Box}{\Box}$$

$$\frac{1}{2} \times \frac{3}{3} = \frac{\Box}{\Box}$$

$$\frac{1}{2} \times \frac{3}{6} = \frac{\Box}{\Box}$$

$$\frac{1}{2} \times \frac{2}{4} = \frac{\Box}{\Box}$$

$$\frac{1}{2} \times \frac{4}{6} = \frac{\Box}{\Box}$$

$$\frac{1}{2} \times \frac{3}{4} = \frac{\Box}{\Box}$$

$$\frac{1}{2} \times \frac{5}{6} = \frac{\Box}{\Box}$$

TRY SOME MORE MULTIPLICATION

Use Fraction Slices™ to solve the equations below.

$$\frac{1}{2} \times \frac{4}{4} = \frac{\boxed{}}{\boxed{}}$$

$$\frac{1}{2} \times \frac{2}{8} = \frac{\boxed{}}{\boxed{}}$$

$$\frac{1}{2} \times \frac{3}{8} = \frac{\boxed{}}{\boxed{}}$$

$$\frac{1}{2} \times \frac{3}{12} = \frac{\boxed{}}{\boxed{}}$$

$$\frac{1}{3} \times \frac{5}{12} = \frac{\boxed{}}{\boxed{}}$$

$$\frac{1}{3} \times \frac{2}{6} = \frac{\boxed{}}{\boxed{}}$$

$$\frac{1}{3} \times \frac{5}{6} = \frac{\boxed{}}{\boxed{}}$$

$$\frac{1}{3} \times \frac{3}{6} = \frac{\boxed{}}{\boxed{}}$$

TRY EVEN MORE MULTIPLICATION

Use Fraction Slices™ to solve the equations below.

$$\frac{2}{3} \times \frac{3}{4} = \frac{\Box}{\Box}$$

$$\frac{1}{3} \times \frac{4}{6} = \frac{\Box}{\Box}$$

$$\frac{1}{2} \times \frac{3}{4} = \frac{\Box}{\Box}$$

$$\frac{1}{3} \times \frac{5}{6} = \frac{\Box}{\Box}$$

$$\frac{1}{3} \times \frac{4}{4} = \frac{\Box}{\Box}$$

$$\frac{1}{3} \times \frac{2}{8} = \frac{\Box}{\Box}$$

$$\frac{1}{3} \times \frac{3}{8} = \frac{\Box}{\Box}$$

$$\frac{1}{3} \times \frac{3}{12} = \frac{\Box}{\Box}$$

MULTIPLY AND SKETCH

- Use Fraction Slices™ to build each problem.

- Count the total of small rectangles for the denominator (put the denominator on the bottom of the fraction).

- Count the overlapped rectangles for the numerator and put it on the top of the fraction.

- Draw the multiplication picture in the squares below.

$$\frac{1}{3} \times \frac{1}{4} = \frac{\square}{\square}$$

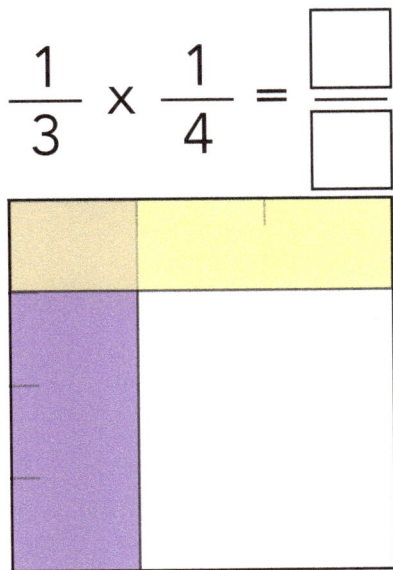

$$\frac{1}{2} \times \frac{1}{6} = \frac{\square}{\square}$$

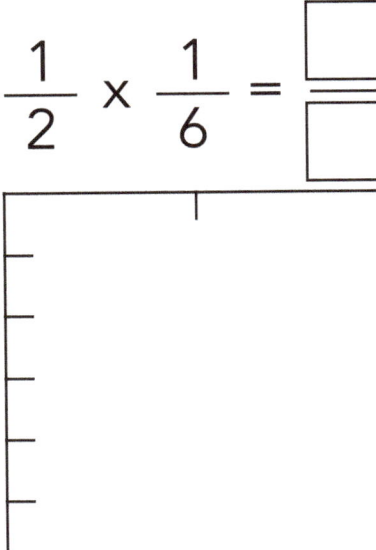

$$\frac{\text{NUMERATOR}}{\text{DENOMINATOR}}$$

$$\frac{1}{2} \times \frac{1}{4} = \frac{\square}{\square}$$

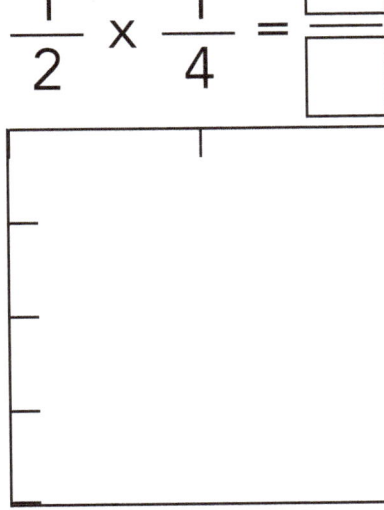

$$\frac{2}{3} \times \frac{1}{4} = \frac{\square}{\square}$$

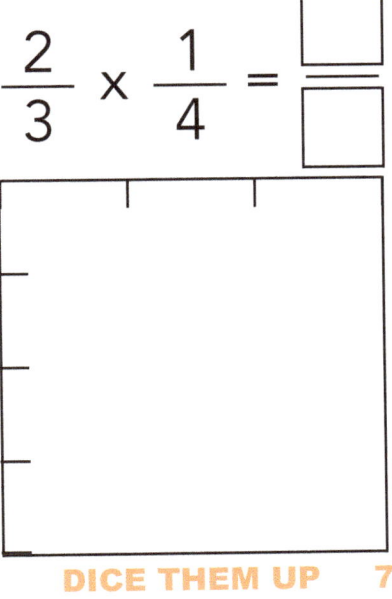

MULTIPLY AND SKETCH

Use the correct color for each fraction. First fraction is vertical, second fraction is horizontal on the grid.
Color the pictorial representation of the answer on the grids below.

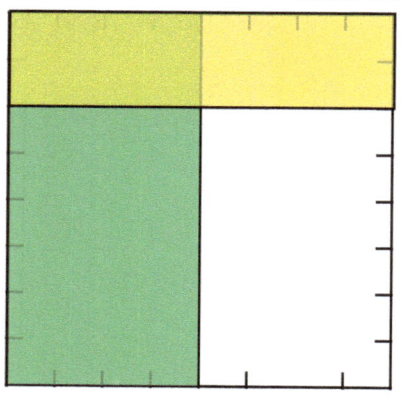

$$\frac{1}{2} \times \frac{1}{4} = \frac{1}{8}$$

$$\frac{5}{6} \times \frac{3}{4} = \frac{}{}$$

$$\frac{3}{8} \times \frac{1}{2} = \frac{}{}$$

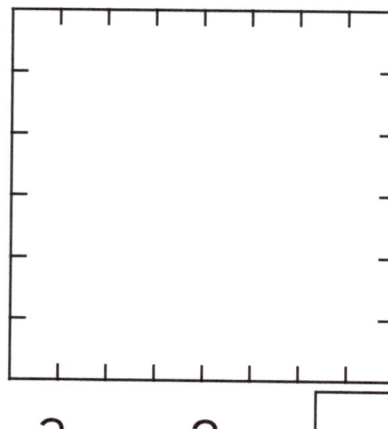

$$\frac{3}{4} \times \frac{2}{3} = \frac{}{}$$

$$\frac{1}{2} \times \frac{3}{4} = \frac{}{}$$

$$\frac{7}{8} \times \frac{1}{4} = \frac{}{}$$

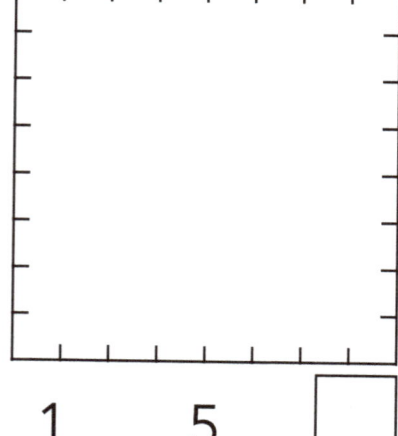

$$\frac{1}{2} \times \frac{5}{8} = \frac{}{}$$

$$\frac{3}{4} \times \frac{3}{8} = \frac{}{}$$

$$\frac{2}{3} \times \frac{7}{8} = \frac{}{}$$

SOLVE THESE SKETCHES

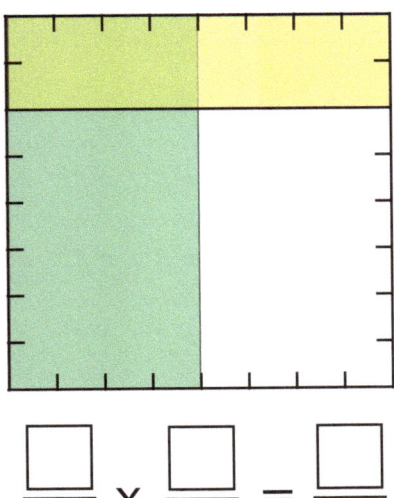

$$\frac{\square}{\square} \times \frac{\square}{\square} = \frac{\square}{\square}$$

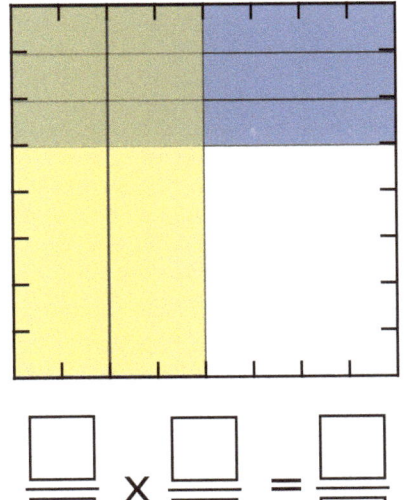

$$\frac{\square}{\square} \times \frac{\square}{\square} = \frac{\square}{\square}$$

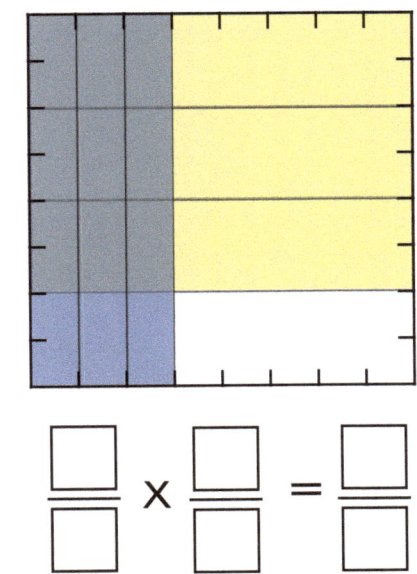

$$\frac{\square}{\square} \times \frac{\square}{\square} = \frac{\square}{\square}$$

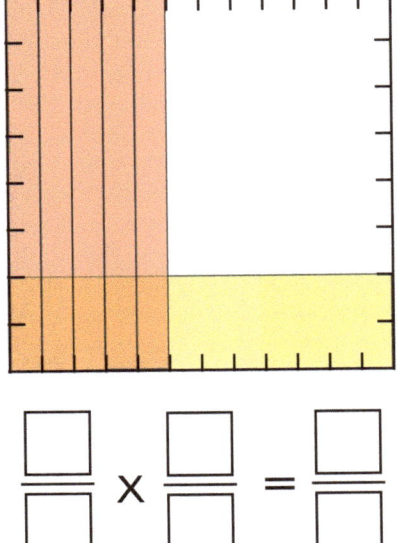

$$\frac{\square}{\square} \times \frac{\square}{\square} = \frac{\square}{\square}$$

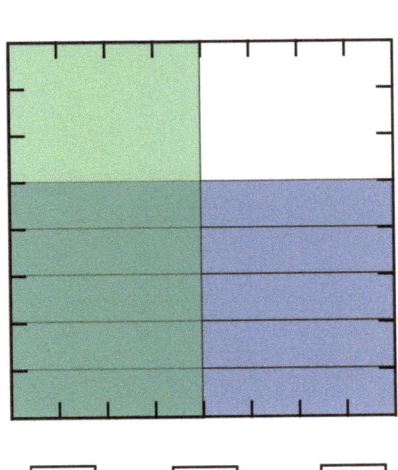
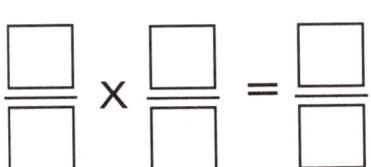

$$\frac{\square}{\square} \times \frac{\square}{\square} = \frac{\square}{\square}$$

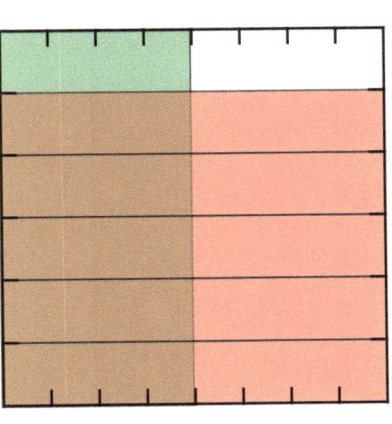
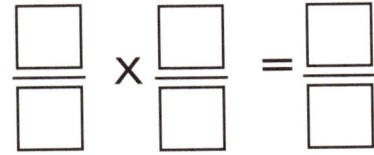

$$\frac{\square}{\square} \times \frac{\square}{\square} = \frac{\square}{\square}$$

SOLVE SOME MORE SKETCHES

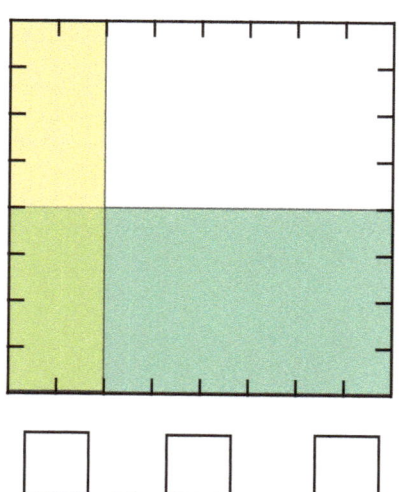

$$\frac{\square}{\square} \times \frac{\square}{\square} = \frac{\square}{\square}$$

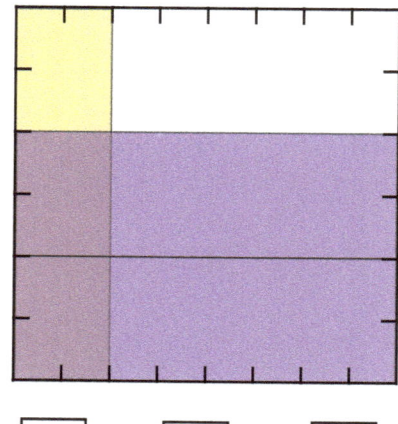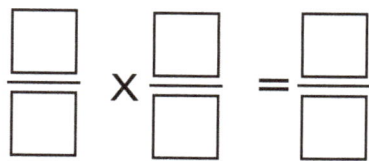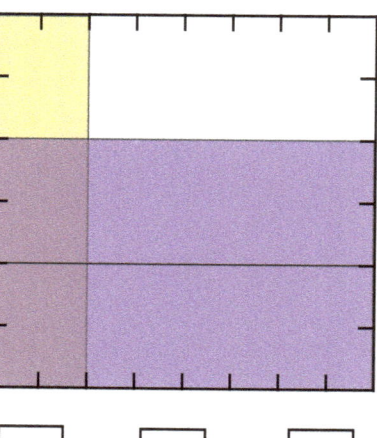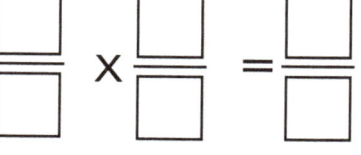

$$\frac{\square}{\square} \times \frac{\square}{\square} = \frac{\square}{\square}$$

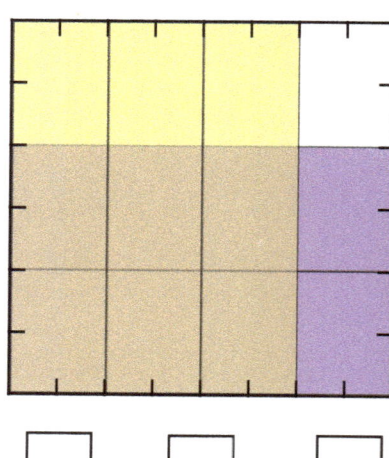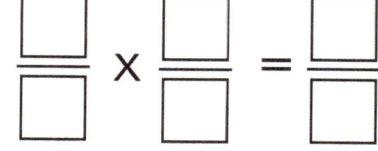

$$\frac{\square}{\square} \times \frac{\square}{\square} = \frac{\square}{\square}$$

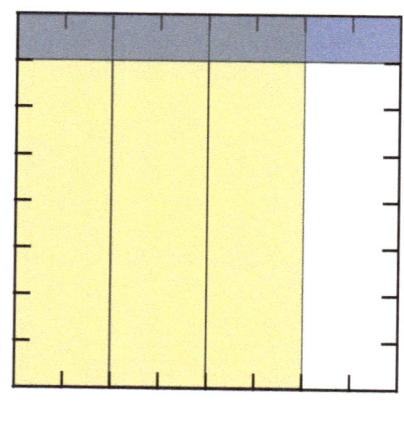

$$\frac{\square}{\square} \times \frac{\square}{\square} = \frac{\square}{\square}$$

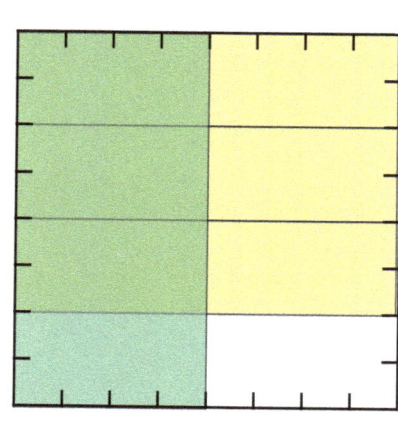

$$\frac{\square}{\square} \times \frac{\square}{\square} = \frac{\square}{\square}$$

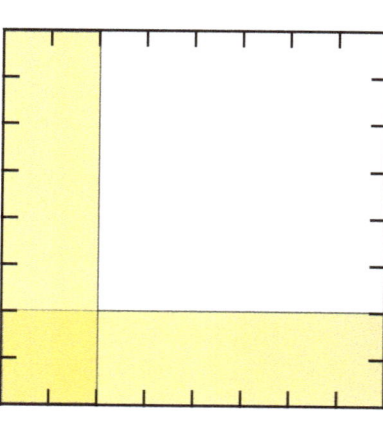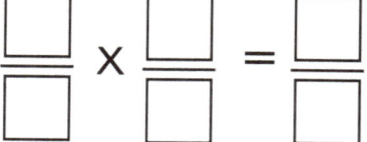

$$\frac{\square}{\square} \times \frac{\square}{\square} = \frac{\square}{\square}$$

SOLVE EVEN MORE SKETCHES

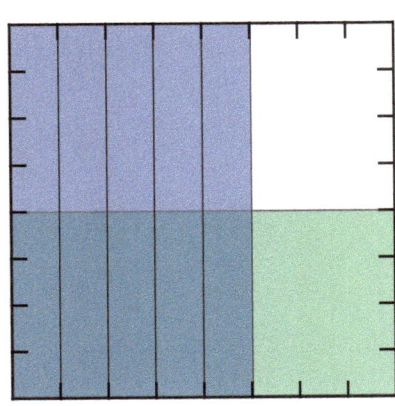

$$\frac{\square}{\square} \times \frac{\square}{\square} = \frac{\square}{\square}$$

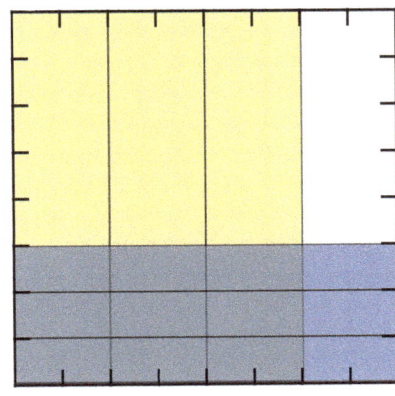

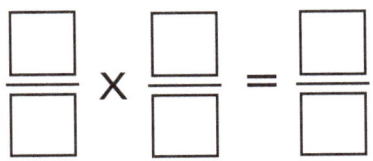

$$\frac{\square}{\square} \times \frac{\square}{\square} = \frac{\square}{\square}$$

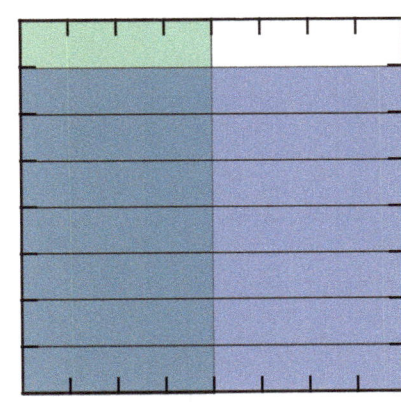

$$\frac{\square}{\square} \times \frac{\square}{\square} = \frac{\square}{\square}$$

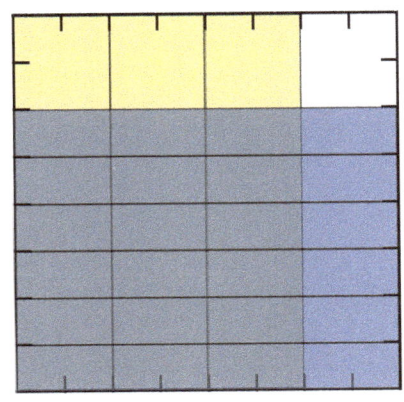

$$\frac{\square}{\square} \times \frac{\square}{\square} = \frac{\square}{\square}$$

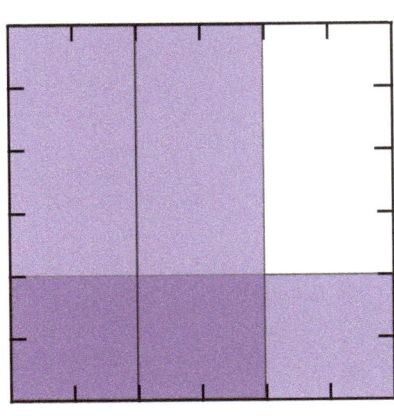

$$\frac{\square}{\square} \times \frac{\square}{\square} = \frac{\square}{\square}$$

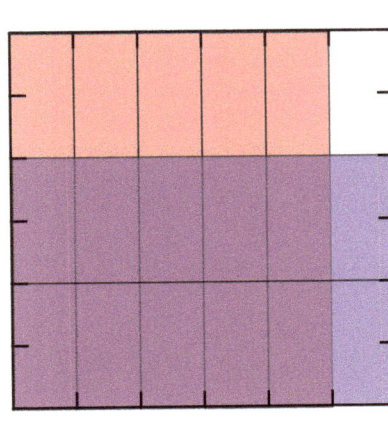

$$\frac{\square}{\square} \times \frac{\square}{\square} = \frac{\square}{\square}$$

MULTIPLICATION TABLE

Use Fraction Slices™ to fill in the multiplication table.
Note: not enough slices for spaces with 'X'.

X	$\frac{1}{2}$	$\frac{1}{3}$	$\frac{1}{4}$	$\frac{1}{6}$	$\frac{1}{8}$	$\frac{1}{12}$
$\frac{1}{2}$	X					
$\frac{1}{3}$		X				
$\frac{1}{4}$			X			
$\frac{1}{6}$				X		
$\frac{1}{8}$					X	
$\frac{1}{12}$						X

COMPLEX DIVISION OF FRACTIONS

Both adults and children can learn so much about fractions with these problems. It is fascinating what students can visualize in their minds after the use of slices to solve the problems. For example, take the problem ½ ÷ ⅓. The ⅓ slice fits into the ½ slice one time and half of the ⅓ slice fits in again. So now we know that ½ ÷ ⅓ = 1 ½.

$$\frac{1}{2} \div \frac{1}{3} =$$

With the problem ⅓ ÷ ½ the question changes because the ½ won't even fit into the ⅓ one time. So the question then becomes, "How <u>much</u> of the ½ slice can fit into the ⅓ slice?" The answer is that ⅔ of the ½ slice fit into the ⅓ slice.

This understanding of fraction division can be learned by almost every student in elementary school grades.

$$\frac{1}{3} \div \frac{1}{2} =$$

Some helpful tips for complex division:

1. Use the slices to determine the answer.

2. When unsure or stumped, it is always okay to look at the answer key and then work backwards to determine how to visualize this answer.

3. Resist the short cut of inverting the divisor and multiplying until the understanding of fraction division is firmly rooted in children's minds.

TRY DIVIDING FRACTIONS

$$\frac{2}{4} \div \frac{1}{4} = \frac{\square}{\square}$$

$$\frac{1}{3} \div \frac{2}{3} = \frac{\square}{\square}$$

$$\frac{1}{8} \div \frac{2}{8} = \frac{\square}{\square}$$

$$\frac{1}{4} \div \frac{2}{4} = \frac{\square}{\square}$$

$$\frac{2}{3} \div \frac{1}{3} = \frac{\square}{\square}$$

$$\frac{1}{8} \div \frac{2}{8} = \frac{\square}{\square}$$

$$\frac{2}{8} \div \frac{5}{8} = \frac{\square}{\square}$$

$$\frac{2}{6} \div \frac{4}{6} = \frac{\square}{\square}$$

$$\frac{2}{12} \div \frac{2}{6} = \frac{\square}{\square}$$

$$\frac{1}{3} \div \frac{1}{2} = \frac{\square}{\square}$$

$$\frac{1}{6} \div \frac{2}{6} = \frac{\square}{\square}$$

$$\frac{5}{8} \div \frac{3}{8} = \frac{\square}{\square}$$

TRY DIVIDING SOME MORE FRACTIONS

$\dfrac{1}{12} \div \dfrac{2}{12} =$ _____

$\dfrac{5}{6} \div \dfrac{1}{6} =$ _____

$\dfrac{1}{8} \div \dfrac{5}{8} =$ _____

$\dfrac{3}{8} \div \dfrac{5}{8} =$ _____

$\dfrac{1}{4} \div 2 =$ _____

$\dfrac{1}{2} \div 2 =$ _____

$2 \div \dfrac{1}{2} =$ _____

$\dfrac{3}{4} \div \dfrac{1}{2} =$ _____

$\dfrac{1}{2} \div \dfrac{3}{4} =$ _____

$\dfrac{1}{2} \div \dfrac{1}{3} =$ _____

$\dfrac{7}{12} \div \dfrac{1}{2} =$ _____

$\dfrac{5}{12} \div \dfrac{1}{2} =$ _____

TRY DIVIDING MORE FRACTIONS

$\dfrac{4}{12} \div \dfrac{2}{3} =$ _____

$\dfrac{1}{12} \div \dfrac{1}{6} =$ _____

$\dfrac{1}{4} \div \dfrac{6}{8} =$ _____

$\dfrac{2}{6} \div \dfrac{2}{3} =$ _____

$\dfrac{1}{4} \div \dfrac{2}{4} =$ _____

$\dfrac{1}{12} \div \dfrac{2}{12} =$ _____

$\dfrac{4}{12} \div \dfrac{8}{12} =$ _____

$\dfrac{1}{3} \div \dfrac{2}{3} =$ _____

$\dfrac{2}{8} \div \dfrac{1}{8} =$ _____

$\dfrac{1}{8} \div \dfrac{3}{8} =$ _____

$\dfrac{3}{8} \div \dfrac{1}{4} =$ _____

$\dfrac{1}{4} \div \dfrac{3}{8} =$ _____

DIVISION PROBLEMS THAT LOOK A LITTLE DIFFERENT

Example: $\frac{1}{6}\overline{)\frac{1}{4}}$ =   is the same as: $\frac{1}{4} \div \frac{1}{6}$ =

$\frac{1}{4}\overline{)\frac{1}{6}}$

$\frac{3}{4}\overline{)\frac{1}{2}}$

$\frac{2}{3}\overline{)1}$

$\frac{3}{4}\overline{)1}$

$\frac{5}{6}\overline{)1}$

$\frac{3}{8}\overline{)2}$

$\frac{5}{6}\overline{)2}$

$\frac{5}{12}\overline{)2}$

FRACTIONS WITH MIXED NUMBERS

COUNTING:

People understand that counting by 1's, and then by 2's, 3's, 4's, etc. can help children understand and gain number sense. Counting by 10's, 100's and 1000's builds further knowledge of place value. This same process of counting works with mixed numerals. Count by ½'s, ⅓'s, ¼'s and so on. The confusion with whole numbers and fractions mixed together usually dissipates with this simple activity. The worksheet provided starts off the process so students can see the pattern then complete it.

ADD, SUBTRACT, MULTIPLY and DIVIDE:

The problems are selected to give students confidence they can combine their knowledge of whole numbers with their newer understanding of fractions in a comfortable way. The problems progress from addition, subtraction, multiplication and division independently, into pages where the operations are combined. The final exam has students using the same pair of numbers for all four operations. A challenge for everyone involved.

UNDERSTANDING MIXED NUMERALS BY COUNTING

$\dfrac{1}{2}$	$\dfrac{1}{3}$	$\dfrac{1}{4}$	$\dfrac{1}{5}$	$\dfrac{1}{6}$
$\dfrac{2}{2} = 1$	$\dfrac{2}{3}$	$\dfrac{2}{4}$	$\dfrac{2}{5}$	$\dfrac{2}{6}$
$\dfrac{3}{2} = 1\dfrac{1}{2}$	$\dfrac{3}{3} = 1$	$\dfrac{3}{4}$	$\dfrac{3}{5}$	$\dfrac{3}{6}$
$\dfrac{4}{2} = 2$	$\dfrac{4}{3} = 1\dfrac{1}{3}$	$\dfrac{4}{4} = 1$		$\dfrac{4}{6}$
$\dfrac{5}{2} = 2\dfrac{1}{2}$	$\dfrac{5}{3} = 1\dfrac{2}{3}$	$\dfrac{5}{4} = 1\dfrac{1}{4}$		$\dfrac{5}{6}$
$\dfrac{6}{2} =$	$\dfrac{6}{3} = 2$			$\dfrac{6}{6} = 1$
$\dfrac{7}{2} =$				
			$\dfrac{10}{5} = 2$	$\dfrac{10}{6} = 1\dfrac{4}{6}$
		$\dfrac{15}{4} = 3\dfrac{3}{4}$		
$\dfrac{16}{2} = 8$				$\dfrac{16}{6} = 2\dfrac{4}{6}$

SOLVING FOR GREATER THAN 1

First find the fractions that equal 1.
Then add the remaining fractions for the total.

EXAMPLE:

$\bigcirc = 1$

$\square = 1$

$\dfrac{1}{4} + \left(\dfrac{1}{2}\right) + \boxed{\dfrac{5}{8}} + \dfrac{1}{4} + \boxed{\dfrac{3}{8}} + \left(\dfrac{1}{2}\right) = 2\dfrac{1}{2}$ or $2\dfrac{2}{4}$

$\dfrac{1}{6} + \dfrac{1}{4} + \dfrac{1}{2} + \dfrac{3}{4} + \dfrac{1}{2} + \dfrac{9}{12} = \underline{\qquad}$

$\dfrac{1}{12} + \dfrac{1}{4} + \dfrac{2}{3} + \dfrac{3}{4} + \dfrac{1}{3} + \dfrac{2}{6} = \underline{\qquad}$

$\dfrac{1}{2} + \dfrac{5}{12} + \dfrac{1}{2} + \dfrac{7}{12} + \dfrac{1}{4} + \dfrac{4}{8} = \underline{\qquad}$

MORE SOLVING FOR GREATER THAN 1

First find the fractions that equal 1.
Then add the remaining fractions for the total.

$$\frac{1}{2} + \frac{7}{12} + \frac{1}{2} + \frac{6}{6} + \frac{5}{12} = \underline{\hspace{2cm}}$$

$$\frac{1}{4} + \frac{2}{4} + \frac{3}{4} + \frac{4}{4} + \frac{1}{4} + \frac{2}{4} + \frac{3}{4} + \frac{4}{4} = \underline{\hspace{2cm}}$$

$$\frac{1}{3} + \frac{2}{3} + \frac{1}{3} + \frac{2}{3} = \underline{\hspace{2cm}}$$

$$\frac{1}{6} + \frac{5}{6} + \frac{3}{6} + \frac{4}{6} + \frac{6}{6} + \frac{1}{6} + \frac{1}{6} + \frac{3}{6} = \underline{\hspace{2cm}}$$

ADDING FRACTIONS

$\dfrac{1}{4} + \dfrac{1}{4} + \dfrac{5}{8} + \dfrac{3}{8} + \dfrac{1}{2} + \dfrac{1}{2} = $ _____

$\dfrac{1}{3} + \dfrac{1}{3} + \dfrac{1}{3} + \dfrac{1}{3} + \dfrac{1}{3} = $ _____

$\dfrac{1}{3} + \dfrac{1}{3} + \dfrac{1}{3} + \dfrac{1}{3} + \dfrac{1}{3} + \dfrac{1}{3} + \dfrac{1}{3} = $ _____

$\dfrac{1}{3} + \dfrac{1}{3} + \dfrac{1}{3} + \dfrac{1}{3} + \dfrac{1}{3} + \dfrac{1}{3} = $ _____

$\dfrac{1}{2} + \dfrac{1}{3} + \dfrac{1}{4} + \dfrac{1}{6} + \dfrac{1}{8} + \dfrac{1}{8} + \dfrac{3}{12} + \dfrac{7}{12} = $ _____

$\dfrac{1}{3} + \dfrac{1}{3} + \dfrac{1}{3} + \dfrac{1}{3} + \dfrac{1}{3} + \dfrac{1}{3} + \dfrac{1}{3} + \dfrac{1}{12} = $ _____

MORE ADDING FRACTIONS

$\dfrac{1}{2} + \dfrac{1}{2} + \dfrac{1}{2} + \dfrac{1}{2} + \dfrac{1}{2} = $ _____

$\dfrac{1}{4} + \dfrac{1}{4} + \dfrac{1}{2} + \dfrac{1}{2} + \dfrac{1}{2} + \dfrac{1}{2} = $ _____

$\dfrac{1}{4} + \dfrac{1}{4} + \dfrac{1}{4} + \dfrac{1}{4} + \dfrac{1}{2} + \dfrac{1}{2} + \dfrac{1}{2} = $ _____

$\dfrac{1}{8} + \dfrac{1}{8} + \dfrac{1}{4} + \dfrac{1}{4} + \dfrac{1}{4} + \dfrac{1}{2} + \dfrac{1}{2} + \dfrac{1}{2} = $ _____

$\dfrac{1}{2} + \dfrac{1}{3} + \dfrac{1}{4} + \dfrac{1}{6} + \dfrac{3}{4} + \dfrac{3}{6} = $ _____

$\dfrac{1}{3} + \dfrac{3}{8} + \dfrac{1}{6} + \dfrac{1}{8} + \dfrac{1}{2} + \dfrac{2}{3} + \dfrac{2}{6} = $ _____

ADDING MIXED NUMBER FRACTIONS

$5 \dfrac{1}{3} + 2 \dfrac{3}{4} = $ _____

$3 \dfrac{2}{3} + 5 \dfrac{1}{2} = $ _____

$6 \dfrac{3}{4} + 1 \dfrac{7}{8} = $ _____

$2 \dfrac{3}{8} + 4 \dfrac{3}{4} = $ _____

$2 \dfrac{3}{4} + 4 \dfrac{3}{8} = $ _____

$2 \dfrac{5}{6} + 4 \dfrac{1}{3} = $ _____

MORE ADDING MIXED NUMBER FRACTIONS

$$7\frac{1}{2} + 6\frac{5}{8} = \underline{\hspace{2cm}}$$

$$70\frac{7}{12} + 60\frac{1}{2} = \underline{\hspace{2cm}}$$

$$700\frac{1}{2} + 600\frac{1}{2} = \underline{\hspace{2cm}}$$

$$2\frac{1}{2} + 1\frac{2}{3} + 3\frac{3}{4} = \underline{\hspace{2cm}}$$

$$2\frac{1}{2} + 1\frac{2}{3} + 4\frac{1}{12} = \underline{\hspace{2cm}}$$

$$2\frac{1}{2} + 1\frac{1}{3} + 1\frac{3}{4} + 3\frac{1}{6} + 1\frac{1}{4} = \underline{\hspace{2cm}}$$

SUBTRACTING MIXED NUMBER FRACTIONS

$1 - \dfrac{1}{3} =$ _____

$1 \dfrac{1}{2} - \dfrac{1}{3} =$ _____

$2 \dfrac{1}{3} - \dfrac{1}{3} =$ _____

$2 \dfrac{1}{2} - \dfrac{2}{3} =$ _____

$3 - \dfrac{1}{3} =$ _____

$3 \dfrac{1}{2} - \dfrac{2}{3} =$ _____

$4 - \dfrac{2}{3} =$ _____

$4 \dfrac{1}{4} - \dfrac{1}{3} =$ _____

$7 \dfrac{2}{3} - 3 \dfrac{1}{2} =$ _____

$7 \dfrac{1}{2} - 3 \dfrac{2}{3} =$ _____

MORE SUBTRACTING MIXED NUMBER FRACTIONS

$4\dfrac{3}{4} - 1\dfrac{1}{2} =$ _____

$4\dfrac{1}{2} - 1\dfrac{3}{4} =$ _____

$6 - \dfrac{1}{2} =$ _____

$6 - 1\dfrac{3}{4} =$ _____

$6 - 1\dfrac{1}{2} =$ _____

$6 - 2\dfrac{2}{3} =$ _____

$6 - 2\dfrac{1}{2} =$ _____

$6 - 3\dfrac{3}{3} =$ _____

$6 - 3\dfrac{1}{2} =$ _____

$6 - 4\dfrac{3}{4} =$ _____

MULTIPLYING WHOLE NUMBERS AND MIXED NUMBER FRACTIONS

(Multiply the whole number by both the other whole number and the fraction)

$2 \times 2\dfrac{1}{2} =$ ___5___

$3 \times 2\dfrac{1}{2} =$ _____

$4 \times 2\dfrac{1}{2} =$ _____

$5 \times 2\dfrac{1}{2} =$ _____

$1 \times \dfrac{5}{2} =$ _____

$2 \times \dfrac{5}{2} =$ _____

$3 \times \dfrac{5}{2} =$ _____

$4 \times \dfrac{5}{2} =$ _____

MORE MULTIPLYING WHOLE NUMBERS AND MIXED NUMBER FRACTIONS

$1 \times 2\dfrac{1}{4} = $ _____

$2 \times 2\dfrac{1}{4} = $ _____

$3 \times 2\dfrac{1}{4} = $ _____

$4 \times 2\dfrac{1}{4} = $ _____

$1 \times \dfrac{9}{4} = $ _____

$2 \times \dfrac{9}{4} = $ _____

$3 \times \dfrac{9}{4} = $ _____

$4 \times \dfrac{9}{4} = $ _____

EVEN MORE MULTIPLYING WHOLE NUMBERS AND MIXED NUMBER FRACTIONS

$1 \times 2\dfrac{1}{3} = $ _____

$2 \times 2\dfrac{1}{3} = $ _____

$3 \times 2\dfrac{1}{3} = $ _____

$4 \times 2\dfrac{1}{3} = $ _____

$1 \times \dfrac{7}{3} = $ _____

$2 \times \dfrac{7}{3} = $ _____

$3 \times \dfrac{7}{3} = $ _____

$4 \times \dfrac{7}{3} = $ _____

DIVIDING MIXED FRACTIONS

$2\dfrac{1}{2} \div \dfrac{1}{2} =$ _____

$2\dfrac{1}{2} \div \dfrac{1}{4} =$ _____

$2\dfrac{1}{2} \div \dfrac{1}{8} =$ _____

$2\dfrac{1}{2} \div \dfrac{1}{3} =$ _____

$2\dfrac{1}{2} \div \dfrac{1}{12} =$ _____

$1\dfrac{1}{3} \div \dfrac{1}{6} =$ _____

$1\dfrac{1}{2} \div \dfrac{1}{4} =$ _____

$1\dfrac{1}{2} \div \dfrac{1}{8} =$ _____

$1\dfrac{1}{2} \div \dfrac{1}{12} =$ _____

$1\dfrac{1}{2} \div \dfrac{1}{6} =$ _____

MORE DIVIDING MIXED FRACTIONS

$$\frac{1}{2} \overline{)\, 2\frac{1}{2}}$$

$$\frac{1}{8} \overline{)\, 2\frac{1}{2}}$$

$$\frac{1}{12} \overline{)\, 2\frac{1}{2}}$$

$$\frac{1}{4} \overline{)\, 2\frac{1}{2}}$$

$$\frac{1}{12} \overline{)\, 5\frac{2}{12}}$$

$$\frac{1}{6} \overline{)\, 1\frac{1}{3}}$$

$$\frac{2}{3} \overline{)\, 16\frac{1}{3}}$$

$$\frac{1}{6} \overline{)\, 2\frac{1}{3}}$$

$$\frac{1}{6} \overline{)\, 3\frac{1}{3}}$$

$$\frac{1}{6} \overline{)\, 4\frac{2}{3}}$$

MULTIPLYING FRACTIONS OF WHOLE NUMBERS

With mixed numbers, think of the 'x' as 'of'.

Example: $\frac{1}{2} \times 2 = 1$ is the same as $\frac{1}{2}$ of $2 = 1$

$\frac{1}{2} \times 4 = $ _____

$\frac{1}{2} \times 6 = $ _____

$\frac{1}{2} \times 8 = $ _____

$\frac{1}{2} \times 10 = $ _____

$\frac{1}{3} \times 1 = $ _____

$\frac{1}{3} \times 2 = $ _____

$\frac{1}{3} \times 3 = $ _____

$\frac{1}{3} \times 4 = $ _____

MORE MULTIPLYING FRACTIONS OF WHOLE NUMBERS

With mixed numbers, think of the 'x' as 'of'.

$\dfrac{1}{4} \times 1 = $ _____

$\dfrac{1}{4} \times 2 = $ _____

$\dfrac{1}{4} \times 3 = $ _____

$\dfrac{1}{4} \times 4 = $ _____

$\dfrac{1}{6} \times 1 = $ _____

$\dfrac{1}{6} \times 2 = $ _____

$\dfrac{1}{6} \times 3 = $ _____

$\dfrac{1}{6} \times 4 = $ _____

EVEN MORE MULTIPLYING FRACTIONS OF WHOLE NUMBERS

With mixed numbers, think of the 'x' as 'of'.

$\dfrac{1}{2}$ x $3\dfrac{1}{2}$ = _____ $\dfrac{1}{2}$ x $5\dfrac{1}{3}$ = _____

$\dfrac{1}{2}$ x $7\dfrac{1}{4}$ = _____ $\dfrac{1}{2}$ x $9\dfrac{1}{6}$ = _____

$\dfrac{1}{3}$ x $6\dfrac{1}{2}$ = _____ $\dfrac{1}{3}$ x $7\dfrac{1}{3}$ = _____

$\dfrac{1}{3}$ x $8\dfrac{1}{4}$ = _____ $\dfrac{1}{3}$ x $9\dfrac{1}{3}$ = _____

PRACTICE ADDING FRACTIONS

Complete the equations below.

$$\frac{1}{3} + \frac{\Box}{\Box} = 1$$

$$\frac{3}{4} + \frac{\Box}{\Box} = 1$$

$$\frac{5}{8} + \frac{\Box}{\Box} = 1$$

$$\frac{5}{8} + \frac{\Box}{\Box} = 1\frac{1}{8}$$

$$\frac{5}{8} + \frac{\Box}{\Box} = 1\frac{1}{4}$$

$$\frac{5}{8} + \frac{\Box}{\Box} = 1\frac{3}{4}$$

PRACTICE SUBTRACTING FRACTIONS

Complete the equations below.

$$1 - \frac{2}{3} = \frac{\boxed{}}{\boxed{}}$$

$$1 - \frac{3}{4} = \frac{\boxed{}}{\boxed{}}$$

$$1 - \frac{5}{8} = \frac{\boxed{}}{\boxed{}}$$

$$1\frac{1}{8} - \frac{5}{8} = \frac{\boxed{}}{\boxed{}}$$

$$1\frac{2}{8} - \frac{5}{8} = \frac{\boxed{}}{\boxed{}}$$

$$1\frac{1}{4} - \frac{5}{8} = \frac{\boxed{}}{\boxed{}}$$

TRY MULTIPLYING AND DIVIDING SOME FRACTIONS

$1 \div \dfrac{1}{3} = \boxed{}$

$1 \times \dfrac{1}{3} = \boxed{}$

$\dfrac{1}{3}\overline{\smash{)}\,1}$ $\boxed{}$

$1 \div \dfrac{2}{3} = \boxed{}$

$1 \times \dfrac{2}{3} = \boxed{}$

$\dfrac{2}{3}\overline{\smash{)}\,1}$ $\boxed{}$

$1 \div \dfrac{3}{3} = \boxed{}$

$1 \times \dfrac{3}{3} = \boxed{}$

$\dfrac{3}{3}\overline{\smash{)}\,1}$ $\boxed{}$

$1 \div \dfrac{1}{4} = \boxed{}$

$1 \times \dfrac{1}{4} = \boxed{}$

$\dfrac{1}{4}\overline{\smash{)}\,1}$ $\boxed{}$

TRY MULTIPLYING AND DIVIDING SOME MORE FRACTIONS

$1 \div \dfrac{2}{4} = \boxed{}$

$1 \times \dfrac{2}{4} = \boxed{}$

$\dfrac{2}{4}\overline{\big)1}$ with box above

$1 \div \dfrac{3}{4} = \boxed{}$

$1 \times \dfrac{3}{4} = \boxed{}$

$\dfrac{3}{4}\overline{\big)1}$ with box above

$1 \div \dfrac{6}{4} = \boxed{}$

$1 \times \dfrac{6}{4} = \boxed{}$

$\dfrac{6}{4}\overline{\big)1}$ with box above

$1 \div \dfrac{8}{4} = \boxed{}$

$1 \times \dfrac{8}{4} = \boxed{}$

$\dfrac{8}{4}\overline{\big)1}$ with box above

TRY MULTIPLYING AND DIVIDING EVEN MORE FRACTIONS

$\dfrac{5}{6} \times \dfrac{1}{2} = \dfrac{\boxed{}}{\boxed{}}$

$\dfrac{3}{8} \div \dfrac{1}{2} = \dfrac{\boxed{}}{\boxed{}}$

$\dfrac{1}{2} \times \dfrac{5}{6} = \dfrac{\boxed{}}{\boxed{}}$

$\dfrac{1}{2} \div \dfrac{3}{8} = \dfrac{\boxed{}}{\boxed{}}$

$\dfrac{5}{12} \div \dfrac{1}{2} = \dfrac{\boxed{}}{\boxed{}}$

$\dfrac{3}{4} \times \dfrac{1}{2} = \dfrac{\boxed{}}{\boxed{}}$

$\dfrac{5}{12} \div \dfrac{5}{6} = \dfrac{\boxed{}}{\boxed{}}$

$\dfrac{2}{2} \times \dfrac{3}{4} = \dfrac{\boxed{}}{\boxed{}}$

MORE PRACTICE MULTIPLYING AND DIVIDING FRACTIONS

$$\frac{7}{8} \div \frac{3}{4} = \frac{\boxed{}}{\boxed{}}$$

$$\frac{9}{12} \div \frac{6}{8} = \frac{\boxed{}}{\boxed{}}$$

$$\frac{3}{8} \div \frac{5}{8} = \frac{\boxed{}}{\boxed{}}$$

$$\frac{1}{4} \times \frac{2}{3} = \frac{\boxed{}}{\boxed{}}$$

$$\frac{1}{4} \times \frac{3}{4} = \frac{\boxed{}}{\boxed{}}$$

$$\frac{2}{12} \div \frac{1}{4} = \frac{\boxed{}}{\boxed{}}$$

$$\frac{9}{12} \div \frac{3}{4} = \frac{\boxed{}}{\boxed{}}$$

$$\frac{2}{3} \times \frac{2}{4} = \frac{\boxed{}}{\boxed{}}$$

MIXED NUMBERS WITH MEASUREMENT

$5\frac{3}{4} + 2\frac{1}{4} =$ _____ $5\frac{3}{4} - 2\frac{1}{4} =$ _____

$\frac{1}{2} \times 5\frac{3}{4} =$ _____ $\frac{1}{4} \times 2\frac{1}{4} =$ _____

$5\frac{3}{4} \div \frac{1}{2} =$ _____ $2\frac{1}{4} \div \frac{1}{4} =$ _____

$5\frac{3}{4}$ hours $5\frac{3}{4}$ hours   1   foot $6\frac{3}{8}$ inches

$- 2\frac{1}{2}$ hours $+ 2\frac{1}{2}$ hours $- 3\frac{3}{4}$ inches $+ 6\frac{1}{4}$ inches

☐ hours   ☐ hours   ☐ inches   ☐ feet

$\frac{1}{3}$ of 1 foot, 3 inches = _____

$2\overline{)\,1\text{ foot, 4 inches}}$

FRACTION OPERATION RELATION

Utilizing the two provided fractions, complete the fraction operation relation table.

A couple answers have been provided as examples.

		+	-	x	÷
1.	$\frac{1}{2}$, $\frac{1}{3}$	$\frac{5}{6}$		$\frac{1}{6}$	
2.	$2\frac{2}{3}$, $1\frac{1}{2}$				
3.	$\frac{7}{12}$, $\frac{1}{2}$				
4.	3, $\frac{3}{8}$				

FRACTION OPERATION RELATION PUZZLE!

One pair of fractions will provide the answers provided in the table when added, subtracted, multiplied and divided correctly. The puzzle is to figure out which two fractions will fit in the first box of each row. No rule or secret is provided. This is essentially a trial and error page until a pair of fractions will create the four answers provided.

	+	-	x	÷
1.		$\frac{5}{6}$	$\frac{1}{6}$	$\frac{1}{6}$	$1\frac{1}{2}$
2.		$\frac{1}{2}$	1	$\frac{1}{16}$	0
3.		$1\frac{1}{2}$		$\frac{10}{18}$	
4.		$\frac{7}{12}$	$\frac{1}{12}$	$\frac{1}{12}$	$1\frac{1}{3}$

THE FINAL: DIVISION AND MULTIPLICATION

$$\boxed{}\ 4\overline{)24}$$

$$\boxed{}\ 6\overline{)24}$$

$$\boxed{}\ 12\overline{)24}$$

$24 \times \dfrac{1}{4} = $ _____

$24 \times \dfrac{1}{6} = $ _____

$24 \times \dfrac{1}{12} = $ _____

$\dfrac{1}{4} \times 24 = $ _____

$\dfrac{1}{6} \times 24 = $ _____

$\dfrac{1}{12} \times 24 = $ _____

$\dfrac{24}{4} = $ _____

$\dfrac{24}{6} = $ _____

$\dfrac{24}{12} = $ _____

THE FINAL:
MORE DIVISION AND MULTIPLICATION

$3 \overline{)24}$ = _____ $8 \overline{)24}$ = _____ $2 \overline{)24}$ = _____

$24 \times \dfrac{1}{3}$ = _____ $24 \times \dfrac{1}{8}$ = _____ $24 \times \dfrac{1}{2}$ = _____

$\dfrac{1}{3} \times 24$ = _____ $\dfrac{1}{8} \times 24$ = _____ $\dfrac{1}{2} \times 24$ = _____

$\dfrac{24}{3}$ = _____ $\dfrac{24}{8}$ = _____ $\dfrac{24}{2}$ = _____

THE FINAL!
ADD, SUBTRACT, MULTIPLY AND DIVIDE

$4 \times 2\frac{1}{2} =$ _____

$2\frac{1}{2} + 4\frac{1}{4} =$ _____

$2\frac{1}{2}\overline{)10} =$ _____

$\dfrac{10}{2\frac{1}{2}} =$ _____

$10 + 2\frac{1}{2} =$ _____

$10 \times \frac{1}{4} =$ _____

$10 \div 4 =$ _____

$\dfrac{10}{4} =$ _____

$10 - 2\frac{1}{2} =$ _____

$7\frac{1}{2} - 2\frac{3}{4} =$ _____

$\frac{1}{3}\overline{)1\frac{2}{3}} =$ _____

$5 \times \frac{1}{3} =$ _____

MATHEMATICS PARADISE!

You have worked hard with students to give them a deep understanding of fractions with a tool called Fraction Slices™. The time spent by both adults and students pays off in the long run. We all know that typically mathematics is taught with short cuts. The academic term is formulas; the common language is "tricks". Over time, most people come to the knowledge that short cuts actually take more time.

The sequence is:

1. Teacher teaches math formulas and has students practice.

2. Students forget the formula.

3. Next year's teacher teaches the formula over with even more practice.

4. Students forget the formula again.

5. The third teacher teaches the formula again.

6. Students forget the formula and tell themselves, "I just am not very good at math".

After experiencing the explanations and problems included in *How to Create Math Experts with Fraction Slices™* you understand that a lot of meaningful instructional time has been spent truly understanding how fractions work with addition, subtraction, multiplication, and division. Your students have more understanding of fractions than almost every adult. Further, they have fractions in their heads and amaze people with their deep understanding. Very nice!

You witnessed the students figuring out the formulas often taught first thing in math classes. Early on they thought, "There is a trick here. As soon as I figure out the trick I do not need the Fraction Slices™!" Thrill enters students' hearts when they discover how to solve problems in their heads without the slices. The long way with deep understanding is actually saving time over the common short cut of teaching formulas first.

Visualizing mathematics in one's head creates mathematicians that memorizing and forgetting will never create. More math experts have been created by you investing time in your students. Your time with Fraction Slices™ is sure to be optimized!

Thank you for joining us in mathematic paradise!

Lyle Lee Jenkins and Peggy McLean

Do you have a great photo or video of your student using one of our products?

We would love the opportunity to share it on our website and social media channels!

Email us at info@ltoj.net

If you have a story to share, we would also like to hear from you. We feature student stories during presentations and on our social media accounts.

Our team loves sharing the joy of a child understanding new concepts. It allows our audience to experience firsthand the mission our team works towards every day; for students to maintain the same love of learning they brought to Kindergarten throughout all their years of schooling and into adulthood.

Thank you for being a loyal customer. We appreciate you!

The LtoJ Team

*Follow us on Instagram, Facebook, TikTok and YouTube
@LtoJLLC*

ABOUT THE AUTHORS

Dr. Lyle Lee Jenkins is an author, speaker, and recognized authority in improving educational outcomes. He believes that implementing a growth mindset and celebrating progress are the keys to helping students learn more and retain their enthusiasm for school.

His education experience spans over 50 years, and ranges from working as a teacher and a principal to a school superintendent and a University Professor. In 2003, Lyle Lee founded LtoJ, LLC hoping to impact and guide the way we approach education.

Lyle Lee Jenkins has authored six books showcasing continuous improvement in schools, including *How to Create a Perfect School*, *Optimize Your School*, *Permission to Forget*, *From Systems Thinking to Systemic Action*, *Improving Student Learning*, and *How to Create a Perfect Home School*. All of his books offer powerful, practical suggestions for every aspect of education. The two most influential people supporting Dr. Jenkins's work are W. Edwards Deming and John Hattie.

Having spoken to educators all across the United States, and into Latin America, Europe, Australia, and Asia, Lyle Lee Jenkins is passionate about equipping the next generation with a true love of learning.

Dr. Lyle Lee Jenkins holds a Bachelor of Arts degree from Point Loma Nazarene University, a Masters of Education from San Jose State University and a Ph.D. from The Claremont Graduate University.

Lyle Lee Jenkins's website, www.LtoJ.net, is a great place to discover useful tools to guide your educational journey.

Peggy McLean is a Math Specialist for elementary age students. She has traveled across the United States training teachers with the use of manipulative materials to build understanding of mathematical concepts. She knows that teachers must first experience the joy of learning and discovering themselves so that they can share this enthusiasm with children. She says, "Teaching is posing problems more than telling students how to do it."

She holds both Bachelor's and Master's degrees from California State University, San Jose. She taught math, science, and social studies courses for pre-service teachers at Notre Dame de Namur University for 25 years.

Peggy was the Elementary Math Specialist at Nueva School for 45 years and has held the same position at Synapse School for the past 8 years. Peggy's expertise in teaching mathematics is well known by audiences at National Council of Teachers of Mathematics conferences as well as those who were fortunate to learn from her in local school district staff development workshops. Educators who hear that Peggy's books are being updated and published for classroom and home education use express joy that her genius work is still available for a new generation of children. Peggy calls San Carlos, California home.

Purchasers of **How to Create Math Experts with Fraction Slices™** may utilize this QR code to download worksheets from this book at no extra cost. This will ease the process of making copies for students. Both the print and digital download versions of this material are protected by copyright laws.

www.ingramcontent.com/pod-product-compliance
Lightning Source LLC
Chambersburg PA
CBHW041515120626
46551CB00018B/2435